Nut Bags and Num-Nums

Nut Bags and Num-Nums

Growing up Rural in Alberta

Lorna Stuber

Copyright © 2023 by Lorna Stuber — Editor, Proofreader, Writer

All rights reserved. No part of this book may be reproduced or transmitted in any form or by any means without written permission from the author.

Cover design: MiblArt

Editor: Kimmy Beach

Book Formatting and Design: Lorna Stuber

ISBN (paperback): 978-1-7778954-4-0

ISBN (ebook): 978-1-7778954-5-7

I have changed and omitted the names of several people in this book to avoid confusion and to protect some people's privacy.

To The Mayor of Taplow, who taught me all the important words.

I miss you every day.

Contents

Introduction	1
The Mayor of Taplow	5
Damn Fine Pencils	10
It Must Be Purple	14
Sisters	21
Do Dogs Go to Heaven?	27
Vermin	30
Greasy Grimy Gopher Guts	34
Pet or Food?	38
Nut Bags	47
The Nuts We Liked	52
The Chuckshot Show	58
The Unwanted Christmas Present	63
Boobies	67
Premature Baldness	72
Chicken Salad Sandwich	78
Learning Useful Words	86
What Clutch?	95
Wilbur	98
Made with Love	103

Eat!	112
Buggy Crocuses and Num-Nums	120
Oodles of Noodles	123
Just Let Me Cut the Damn Apple	129
The Guitar Man	134
The Lutherans	146
Headless Criminals and Fried Chicken	149
The Kids'll Be Fine	158
Shitty Pie à la Mode	164
All Thumbs	176
I Found My Voice	179
The Hallowed Weenies	187
Welcome, Friend. Goodbye, Friend	193
Gay	200
Death is Toast	203
The Cowfur Mobile	214
We Felt Seen	219
Curfew	231
Rapscallions	243
The Bizarre Bazaar	253
We Knew	257
Afterword	260

Introduction

I'm from Hanna, and no, I don't know Nickelback.

When meeting new people, I used to say, "I grew up on a farm ten miles outside of Hanna," but as soon as they heard Hanna, they immediately responded with, "Do you know Nickelback?" So now I save them the trouble.

I am a few years older than the members of Nickelback, and I was a farm kid. They were town kids. It's not that farm kids and town kids didn't mix when I was growing up. Those of us who were in school together did. But "the boys," as my friend Laura calls them (she claims to be their biggest fan), were younger than me by enough years that we weren't in junior or senior high school together. The kids I knew best were within two years of me in school. I also formed tight bonds with our neighbours' kids regardless of their ages.

No, I didn't—and still don't—know Nickelback (sorry, Laura, I can't get you those backstage passes), but I had Lanny MacDonald's mother as a substitute teacher in junior high school. And in my first off-the-farm job working at the cattle auction in Hanna on Saturdays, Lanny's uncle was one of the men working in the back penning the cattle. I guess I'm almost famous, after all.

There's a certain camaraderie among neighbours in rural prairie communities. And those of us who grew up in those settings can certainly relate to others who have done so even if their stomping grounds may have been hundreds of miles away.

My younger cousin Darren grew up in Calgary and was always interested in our farm life. When his parents brought him and his brother to visit, he drilled my dad with questions about farming, the cattle, the horses, and daily chores. I had a suspicion he would have rather been on the farm with us than in the city. And conversely, I was always slightly jealous of him and his brother for the opportunities they had but we didn't have in small-town Alberta: having more options at school for subjects like Music, Drama, and foreign languages; being able to go to movies when they were released; and being able to walk out the front door and play with neighbours. Hanna had one movie theatre when I was growing up, and the movies came to town two or three months after they were released. The theatre has since closed down and the town doesn't have one any more.

I had lots of friends, but we were at least five miles from the closest farm. Play time with other kids always coincided with my parents' visits with their friends or get-togethers to help each other with farming or ranching duties.

But one of the biggest advantages of growing up rural is that sense of community. Since I was a teenager, I have always said, "My mom knew what I was up to in town on a Friday night before I even did," because the phone lines were hot and parents looked out for each other's kids. Plus, don't people love to gossip? Everyone knowing your business can be a positive or a negative; the positive is that those in the community support your hobbies, encourage your pursuits, and cheer you on in your victories. Those relationships can make one feel like they have a huge extended family supporting them through all of life's challenges. You don't have to become famous for your home community to support and be proud of you.

Thirty-five years after moving away, I still have those relationships. I keep in touch with many of my parents' friends and several of my childhood friends and their parents. A sense of belonging bubbles up when I am in my hometown and someone I haven't seen in thirty years recognizes me and stops to catch up. I've had several of these types of conversations since I moved away from home:

"You're Lorna Stuber, aren't you?" the local person asks me.

"Yes! Hi, how are you?"

"I remember when you were only 'this tall'. Where are you living these days?"

"Okotoks."

"Are you still teaching?"

"No, I resigned a few years ago and retrained. Now, I'm running my own business as an editor and writer."

"Oh, that sounds really interesting! You look so much like your mom."

"Aw, thank you! I take that as a great compliment! She was a great lady."

Nut Bags and Num-Nums

"Yes, she was. We used to buy cream off of her when your parents were still on the farm. How is your dad doing? And where is he living now?"

Sometimes I'm embarrassed that I walk away from the conversation asking myself, *Who the heck was that?* It's easy to forget people you don't see for decades, but I look a lot like both my mom and dad, so people recognize me when they see me. I recognize faces, but I have a hard time recalling names at times.

I've lived in in the jungles of Peru and the suburbs of Tokyo. I have travelled the world: Easter Island, China, Australia, Egypt, Iceland, the Caribbean, Jordan, various countries in Europe, and many more. But I've always been quick to tell people, regardless of where I live and where I travel, my roots and my heart will aways be in Alberta and with its people.

The Mayor of Taplow

When my dad was in his eighties, declining due to the aftereffects of a stroke and increasing struggles with dementia, I came full circle. I felt like I was back to my childhood days of spending hours together in silence ... both of us just "being." It was at that point, of course, a role reversal. I was the one parenting: taking him to the ER when he had health emergencies, feeding him when he could no longer feed himself, taking him for drives when he could no longer drive, taking him for or bringing him treats: ice cream, chocolate, or his beloved "Tim's" coffee and a donut.

On the last day I saw him, I cried, knowing I was spending my last minutes with him. I gave him a hug and told him, "It's okay, Dad. You can go and be with Mom now."

As I leaned over him in his bed and hugged him, even though he was sleeping, he turned his head toward me and his cheek brushed against mine ... just as it used to when I was a little girl. I had always loved sitting on his lap while he rubbed his scruff against my cheek, giggling because I was so ticklish.

My dad was a man of few words. His moments of silence, including those last few minutes I spent with him, always said more to me than any words he could have uttered. That moment, on the last day I saw him, I know that turning his head toward me in his sleep was his way of saying his goodbye to me.

Nut Bags and Num-Nums

***

When I was growing up, Mom always called my dad The Mayor of Taplow. I was in my teens when I learned why.

Train tracks ran through the section of land we owned south of our farmyard. Until the train stopped running in the late 1980s, I could hear it from my bedroom as it passed by about a mile away.

Taplow was a railway siding—a place along railroad tracks named so that rail workers know exactly where they need to go when work needs to be done on a certain section of the rail line.

The closest farm to ours, which I could see out of my bedroom window, is about two miles away across country. To get from our farmstead to theirs though requires driving on two different highways for fifteen minutes. Taplow was nothing but a sign beside the railroad tracks, in the middle of the prairie, halfway between our farm and theirs.

When I was in my thirties, I took a friend to my parents' farm for a visit.

"My dad is The Mayor of Taplow," I told her.

"Taplow? What's that?" she asked.

"We'll show you!"

Dad drove us out to the railroad sign so she could see Taplow for herself. While we were on our excursion, we had to wait for someone driving a tractor along the only "road" (a trail that was carved into the prairie pasture from Dad driving the truck to check cattle) until we could continue on our way.

I told her, "This is rush hour in Taplow."

My dad was originally a city kid, but he spent the majority of his life farming and ranching on the Alberta prairie. He raised his cattle and horses with care and pride.

He was proud to be part of the Alberta beef industry, and although he always ate anything Mom put in front of him, he made no bones about the fact that he preferred beef, even over chicken or pork.

Mom loved lamb, and though she could never convince Dad to get a few lambs to keep on the farm, she bought some lamb meat now and then as a treat for herself. She tried to fool Dad by not telling him what it was; she thought she could get it past him, but not so.

"This is SHEEP!" he always proclaimed after one bite.

Mom had an overabundance of zucchini most years and put it in anything and everything to use it up. One recipe she tried was for lemon meringue pie, one of my dad's favourites. I couldn't taste the zucchini in the filling but we could see tiny flecks of it.

"I can see the zucchini in this," he muttered, poking at the pie with his fork as he inspected it.

***

My dad had a grade ten education. He was good at math, taking out a pen and paper whenever he needed to do calculations of potential expenses. He scratched everything out on paper. "Figgerin'" was what he called it.

And he loved to read. As a young girl who was quickly growing passionate about reading and writing, I was excited that my dad shared this interest with me. For decades, my sister and I each went out in search of new books as Christmas gifts every year to encourage him to keep reading. Every fall, we looked to see if a hockey player, country music performer, or Western novelist had a new book out. He especially loved biographies of his heroes: hockey players, country singers, and other farmers and ranchers who had led interesting lives, particularly those who helped establish the ranching business in the West.

When I was a kid, there wasn't a Girl Guides or Brownies club in Hanna, but the Alliance Church had a Pioneer Girls group. Pioneer Girls was sort of a Christian version of these two groups. We learned arts and crafts, biblical stories and lessons, and some life skills.

One of the events that Pioneer Girls held one winter evening was Father-Daughter Night. I wasn't going to invite my dad because I figured he'd be too busy to go. I was used to having Mom take us to events because Dad was always so busy on the farm. And regardless of the season, Dad also rarely accompanied us to church, so I didn't think he would come. But he did! Among other activities that night, we worked together pulling taffy until it was good and soft, and then we enjoyed eating the taffy together.

Nut Bags and Num-Nums

I was in my teens when I took note of my dad's eating manners. He was cattle rancher—a man who worked with animals, machinery, and his hands, and so one would think he was rough around the edges. Quite the contrary. His demeanour was calm, quiet, and gentle—except when he lost his cool and used his "words".

But one day I noticed how he ate, and after that, I snuck a peek every now and then. Yes, his table manners were consistent. If I'm cutting a steak or piece of chicken, I am not exactly refined. I make a fist around my fork with my right hand, stab the meat with the fork, and saw pieces of it off with the knife in my left hand. Then, I switch my fork and knife to the opposite hand and eat (I'm left-handed). Not my dad. He always kept both hands palm down facing the table, and he cut his meat slowly and properly, as if he were dining with royalty. I was impressed that somewhere along the way my grandmother must have taught him to eat with good manners and that these manners stuck with him.

He also hated to get his fingers sticky and ate his Tim Hortons donut with a knife and fork if they were available. I always assumed that he didn't want to eat with his hands because he worked manual labour outside and his hands were often in the muck, mud, manure, or inside or on an animal. It may have simply been because he felt that eating with his hands was improper.

My sister and I describe Dad as a simple man, but he was complex in his own way. His love of ranching and of working the land created a foundation that provided us a fun and free childhood.

Damn Fine Pencils

My dad's parents bought our farm when he was a teenager because he wanted to pursue ranching and farming. When he and my mom got married, they took over the farm and began to build their lives together.

"We had no money when we first got married, so we used apple crates for furniture," my mom told me. "That's what we used for a table and chairs until we could afford real ones."

Almost a year and a half after my parents married, they had my sister. Janice was born in early May; my mom became a mother on Mother's Day. A little more than four years later, I was born a couple of days after Labour Day.

"I was baking apple pies when I went into labour with you. It was getting close to harvest, and I wanted some pies in the freezer for when your dad and grandpas started harvest. And you were born five days late."

I'm a habitual procrastinator, so I guess stalling was in my nature even when I was in the womb. One of my mom's nicknames for me was Last-Minute Lorna.

"I was happy to have another daughter. I expected I would get a lot of help in the house," she told me when I was a teenager.

But I foiled her plans. My sister, being much more gregarious than I am, was almost always the center of attention.

Nut Bags and Num-Nums

I was often forgotten or overlooked because I was quiet, and I preferred to keep to myself. I used this personality difference to my advantage. When the three of us were in the house and Mom got us started doing household chores or working on something together in the kitchen, the first chance I got when her back was turned or her attention was on Janice, I slipped out the door, found my dad, and followed him around.

When I was old enough to saddle and ride my horse unaccompanied, if my dad was in the field dealing with crops or doing other work I couldn't help him with, I saddled up and rode off for hours. I loved exploring the flowers and rocks, looking for snails along the creek, and scouring the horizon for rabbits or coyotes.

"My mom never worried about me when I rode off for hours," I told a co-worker a few years ago. "She knew I'd come back eventually—when my ass got sore from too many hours in the saddle or when I was hungry."

"You were a feral child?" he asked me.

"Ha! I've never thought of it that way, but I guess, yeah, I kinda was."

Yes, Janice and I are as opposite as two people can be.

"I was the chatty, outgoing, and rebellious one, and you were always shy and quiet and obedient," she often says to me.

She relayed the following story to me:

"I couldn't have been much older than five when Dad took me to town, probably to give Mom and you a break from me.

Nut Bags and Num-Nums

He was doing his business with the grain elevator guy and while I was sitting there, I spotted a container filled with bright-yellow, sharp, pointy pencils. Dad had asked me to keep quiet, but I was a yappy child. Finally, I couldn't stay quiet any longer so I blurted to the elevator guy, 'Those are sure nice pencils!' Of course he gave me a mittful of pencils, which I proudly took home. That story became one that Dad teased me about for years. You would have been able to sit there for hours without saying a word. Not me."

"I would have been too terrified to speak in front of another adult," I replied.

"Yeah, what's with that? You were always too scared to talk in front of anyone other than Mom and Dad."

I avoided eye contact anytime I was walking down the street with Mom and someone approached from the other direction. Even when others said hello to me, I responded with a half smile and continued to avoid eye contact. Strangers who asked my name often thought I said "Laura" because I mumbled my response while staring at the sidewalk.

I also ran in fear whenever I was playing in the yard and heard a vehicle approaching. If I knew it wasn't my dad, I took off and hid, peeking out from behind the garage, the chicken coop, a hay stack, or the tack shed to see who it was. Only after knowing who had come did I decide whether to make an appearance or not.

A complete stranger? *No way.*

Grandparents or other family members? *Ok, I'll come out.*

Nut Bags and Num-Nums

Family friends and neighbours? Whether I stayed hidden depended on who it was and how comfortable I felt with them.

I got into trouble daily for not saying "present" during roll call in grade one. In spite of my shyness, I would have been fine with saying "here" or "yes" when my name was called during roll call but to me, "present" meant "gift". I thought it was a stupid word to reply with when the teacher called out attendance. But we were to reply with "present." Nothing else.

I never responded. My teacher threatened with marking me absent, but I didn't care. I knew I was there. My parents knew I was there, and my teacher knew I was there. I called her bluff. I never got in trouble for being "absent" (because I never was), but I was constantly reprimanded for not saying "present" when called on. My classmates teased me about this well into elementary school until I started to talk to them.

"Your teachers used to talk to me at parent-teacher interviews about how you refused to speak at school," Mom told me when I was in my twenties. "They asked if you were like that at home, too. Some of them thought maybe you had some sort of mental handicap or emotional problems."

"Feral children lack the basic social skills [and] ... display a complete lack of interest in the human activity around them."[1]

Hmm ...

---

[1] "Wikipedia: Feral child." Wikimedia Foundation. Last updated August 7, 2023. 15:44. wikipedia.org/wiki/Feral_child.

It Must Be Purple

Our original farmhouse had two bedrooms, a living room, one bathroom, and a kitchen and small dining area combined on the main floor. The basement was partially developed; about half of it was not, with dirt floors and a room where my parents stored coal for the furnace. The one room that was developed had a set of bunk beds. Every summer, Janice and I were excited about moving downstairs for a few months. We had our own private area of the house down there. In the spring, we hauled our toys downstairs and played for hours each day before settling in to sleep on the bunk beds in the coolness of the basement. Having that as our bedroom for a few months was like being at summer camp without leaving home. And what kid doesn't love bunk beds?

In the winter, we shared a bed in the smaller bedroom upstairs, across the living room from our parents' room. The intimate space became problematic when I got to be old enough to annoy my sister and we started our typical sibling fights. To conclude the first fight I remember having with her, Janice drew an imaginary line through the middle of the room with her foot.

"This is where the room divides into your side and my side," she told me.

She was standing a few inches into her side of the room, which contained the bed. My side had the door. The segregation lasted a few hours.

Nut Bags and Num-Nums

As much as I loved those bunk beds in the basement and having our own section of the house down there, I was ecstatic when my parents decided they were going to build a new house on the farm. I was going to get my own room!

I was four when the planning and construction began. Mom and Dad went to Hanna to look at blueprints. I sat silently beside them while they flipped through a colour catalogue, looking the different options and talking to the designer.

They narrowed it down to four options.

"We have to build this one," I whispered to my mom as I pointed to one of the pictures on our second last visit.

I was convinced we needed the fourth house—the pink house ... because it was *pink*. My parents ignored my edict and selected the floor plan they thought would best suit our family of four.

My dad, grandpas, and neighbours built the house with help from electricians and other professional tradesmen from town.

I had lost the battle when it came to building the pink house, but I was determined to get my way when it came to designing my new bedroom. It was going to be *my* room—one that I would never have to share with anyone—so my four-year-old stubborn self insisted that the room be purple. After weeks of whining and begging, I wore my parents down. They relented and I got my beloved room: dark purple carpets with lilac-coloured paint on the walls. After we moved in, my grandma bought into my vision and made me a purple Holly Hobby quilt. Almost fifty years later, that quilt is on my spare bed.

Nut Bags and Num-Nums

My parents hosted a housewarming party and invited everyone who helped as well as other neighbours and friends. As I sat on my dad's lap, I knew that the stubby brown glass bottle he was holding contained something that only adults drank. Curious as to what this forbidden liquid was, I wrapped my fingers around the bottle, slowly pulling it toward my mouth. He lifted the bottle to my lips and tilted it back, allowing me a small sip.

This tastes good! Why aren't kids allowed to drink it? I wondered.

I waited a few moments and then silently requested more. He complied a couple more times before cutting me off.

One of our neighbours had a little too much of that delicious liquid and somehow got his hands on my mom's rag mop, claiming this as his new "skinny hippy girlfriend" and dance partner for the rest of the night.

The guests brought gifts. As Mom was opening one package, I said to her, "I sure hope it's a box of chocolates!" A couple of neighbours laughed at me. It was a bottle of whiskey.

I had my own purple bedroom with a door that I could lock. I was thrilled that I could isolate myself and play with my dolls. As I got older, I locked myself in my room and lay on my bed, reading for hours. I was obsessed with devouring any book I could get my hands on. The only problem with my room was that it was down the hallway from my parents' room so at night, they could always see light peeking out from under my door.

I fell in love with books long before I could read. Some of my earliest memories are of going into town with my mom on a

Nut Bags and Num-Nums

Saturday morning and visiting the library. The following Saturday, we returned the books we had chosen the previous week and got new ones. Sometimes we renewed the books I loved so I could hear them over and over.

When I was old enough, Mom allowed me to pick my own books. Even though I couldn't yet read them, I knew what my favourites were by the pictures on the covers. One series that I was loved was the *Ant and Bee* books, by Angela Banner. Ant and Bee had seemingly endless stories to tell about their friendship and the fun activities they did together. Over time, we checked out every *Ant and Bee* book that the Hanna library had, and when we had made our way through all of them, we started over.

Another favourite was *The Monster at the end of this Book: Starring Lovable, Furry Old Grover from Sesame Street*. The first time my mom read this book to me, I was terrified of what the monster at the end of the book looked like and what it would do. Once I knew the ending, I begged her to read it to me again and again. Each time I heard the story, my fear decreased a bit more. It wasn't until she had read it to me five or six times that I realized the ending was not going to change and that [SPOILER ALERT] the monster at the end of the book was going to be lovable furry old Grover himself *every time we finished the book*. This was one of the first books I owned. And when I was able to read, I read it time and time again, giggling each time I got to the not-so-scary ending.

The best part of my first couple of years in that new house was time spent sitting or lying beside my mom while she sat on my bed reading to me. I watched her flip the pages of the books I chose, listening to her tell me the stories of the characters on

Nut Bags and Num-Nums

those pages. I allowed her voice to take me away to places the characters lived, to images I created in my mind.

"Time for bed, Lorna. Crawl under the covers and I will read to you. What book do you want me to read tonight?"

"*Around the World with Ant and Bee* please."

I nestled into the covers while Mom read and showed me the pictures.

"Ant and Bee had a lovely time in Australia, and they played with kangaroos! Then a man in Australia told Bee to look for his lost umbrella in another large land called South America."[2]

I looked at the picture showing Ant and Bee playing with the kangaroos. I had no idea where Australia was, and I had never seen a kangaroo.

Kangaroos. What are kangaroos like? Are they soft like puppies and kittens? How big are they? What kind of games can you play with a kangaroo? I wonder if I will ever get to see a kangaroo.

Once I was old enough to read, I defied my mom's orders to go to sleep at 7:00pm. Especially in the summer when the sun was up well past 10:00pm, I felt it was unfair that I was expected to close my eyes and try to sleep when there were books to read. When she sent me to bed during those bright summer evenings, I flew away to other places—the worlds within my books.

---

[2] Banner, Angela. *Around the World with Ant and Bee.* Farshore. 2021. p. 57-58.

Nut Bags and Num-Nums

I longed to be friends with Alec Ramsay, the boy who acquired a majestic, coal-black Arabian stallion in Walter Farley's *The Black Stallion* series. When Alec travelled through and eventually raced The Black (Shetan) in the Arabian desert in the second book, I dreamed about that part of the world: Arabia. Even the word sounded fascinating and exciting. I imagined the dark-skinned people adorned with flowing robes and head coverings, racing those beautiful Arabian horses over sawdust-like sand.

The race is about to start. I'm on a grey Arabian horse, and Alec is to my right riding The Black. There's nothing in front of us but miles and miles of tan-coloured sand. Not even any footprints in the sand. It's like being on the moon—going where no one has gone before.

"READY, SET, GO!" *the man to my left in the white flowing robe shouted.*

We're off! Racing through the sand in Arabia! The dry, hot wind is blowing, and our horses are kicking up sand as they gallop full speed ahead! Alec is right beside me. All the other jockeys are falling behind. We're really pulling ahead!

I owned every book in *The Black Stallion* series. I had either bought them with my allowance or asked for the ones I was missing as Christmas presents. I read them all multiple times.

I did the same with the *Anne of Green Gables* series.

I have beautiful, long, flowing auburn hair, just like Anne.

(My natural hair colour had red highlights that revealed themselves when I spent my summers in the sun.)

When I grow up, I'm going to marry a nice boy like Gilbert, and I'm going to become a teacher, just like Anne.

What does raspberry cordial taste like, I wonder?

My books became an extension of my reality: limitless freedom in the wind and the blue sky, with horses and other animals as my best friends. I began to live in my imagination and dream of my future.

Sisters

Janice was always, shall we say, a little less compliant than I was. I was obedient because I was terrified of getting into trouble. Even though I had a strong will, the push-back always occurred inside my mind until I got older. I rarely talked back and I tried my best to be well-behaved.

When Janice was in elementary school and I was still at home, she and her best friend, Maryanne, cooked up a plan. Maryanne's dad worked for the railroad. Her family lived on the outskirts of town in a house provided by the railway company, so she was on the bus route with the farm kids.

When the bus stopped to drop off Maryanne after school one day, her mom was waiting on the road with a box, which she gave to Janice. Thirty minutes later, my sister got off the bus at home toting this box.

"Mom! Look what I got!"

She proudly opened the box to reveal a tabby kitten.

"Where did you get that?" Mom asked.

"From Maryanne. Her cat had kittens."

"Why did you bring that home without asking me? We don't need a new cat. You should have asked before you brought this thing home."

But the deal had been done. The kitten stayed, and Janice named her Ears.

Ears grew to be one of the best farm cats any farm family could ever hope for. She lived a good fifteen years catching truckloads of mice, having boatloads of kittens, and being a docile, friendly children's pet. She was Janice's cat, but I got the odd scratch in behind her ears.

One of her brood was a kitten my sister named after one of her favourite musicians: Billy Joel. Yes, that was the cat's full, name, but we just called him Billy. By the time Billy entered our lives, my sister was in her early teens and decided that the program would change: Billy should be a house cat. We both brought him in now and then, and he was well-behaved and calm the house.

He was, however, terrified of the vacuum cleaner. Whenever one of us started it up in the room he was in, he sprinted off for any other part of the house.

Janice had a plan.

"Let's cure him of his fear of vacuum cleaners. If we make him listen to the vacuum cleaner close-up, he'll learn that it's not going to hurt him."

"Okay," said the obedient one.

We were playing in the basement. She brought the vacuum cleaner into the family room.

"Plug in the vacuum cleaner. I'll grab Billy."

Nut Bags and Num-Nums

I did as she instructed while she picked up the cat. Then, with both hands, she pressed him against the top of the worm-like canister. I turned it on.

"YYEEEEEOOOOOOWWWWWWLLLLL!"

Billy fought and squirmed and wrestled until he broke free. He took off in a streak of black-and-white fur for parts unknown.

Janice turned off the vacuum cleaner.

"Let's go find him."

"Here Billy. Here Billy Billy Billy," we both called.

He was having none of it. Wherever he was, he was *not* resurfacing.

We finally found him upstairs in the living room hiding under the couch next to a large pile of kitty poo. The vacuum cleaner had literally scared the shit out of him. It wasn't easy or pleasant to clean up the runny mess, which was our responsibility since we were the cause of it.

We never again tried to cure him of his fear of the vacuum cleaner.

***

Janice and I never got into fist fights. Most of our conflict consisted of typical sibling bickering and squabbling. But her one physical form of control over me was tortuous. She quickly learned that the best way to render me helpless was to pin me to the ground and tickle me until I couldn't breathe.

Nut Bags and Num-Nums

"STOP! AHHHHSTOP! HELPMEHELPME!" I shouted between shrieks and giggles and gasps for air while writhing away. Even though I knew escape was impossible, I still tried to break free. With the almost four-and-a-half-year age difference, she had no trouble overpowering me.

I knew this was her way of teasing me, just as my uncles and grandpa also often tickled me, but unlike them, she was merciless. When she finally released me from her torment, I always had to lay on the ground for a minute to catch my breath.

Another time she exerted her power over me was when our family was on the way home from the circus in Hanna. My parents had bought me a balloon, and I was clutching the string of my treasured memento of the fun day. Of course no one used seat belts or car seats for kids. My sister and I were messing around in the back seat squabbling.

"Your feet are on my side of the seat," I said to my sister.

"So?"

"So, get your feet away from me."

"Make me."

I pushed her feet away with one hand, but she moved them back.

"Stop it! Mom, make her stop," I whined.

"Stop fighting, you girls," Mom said. Dad was silent, as usual.

Nut Bags and Num-Nums

"What's it to you if I put my feet over there? They're not touching you."

"Because it's my side of the car," I replied.

On and on we went until Janice finally had enough of me. She opened the car window on her side, snatched the balloon I was holding, pushed it out the window, and rolled the window back up. I watched my balloon float away.

The rest of the ride home was silent as I slumped into the corner against the car door and pouted.

She still owes me a balloon.

***

When Mom and Dad went to a wedding or other social events and left us at home, we had babysitters until Janice was old enough to look after the two of us. I always felt like she enjoyed taking advantage of her position of power to boss me around.

"Go get the eggs out of the hen house."

"Feed the cats."

"Go clean your room before Mom and Dad get home."

One night she was sitting on the couch reading her book.

"It's your turn to do the dishes," she told me.

I'd had enough.

Nut Bags and Num-Nums

Why do I have to do the dishes while she sits and reads? Mom and Dad can boss me around, but she can't.

I silently went into the kitchen but no, not to do the dishes. I opened a drawer, carefully selected the biggest butcher knife I could find, and closed the drawer.

I stood behind the drawer holding the knife up as she continued reading on the couch in the living room.

"If you boss me around one more time, I'm gonna kill you," I said, glaring at her, holding the knife upright.

She looked at me for a moment and slowly turned back to her book. She didn't say another word to me that night.

I was in bed when Mom and Dad got home, so I never heard the conversation she had with them, but my butt told me loud and clear what that conversation would have been about. That incident prompted my dad to take off his belt the next day. My tiny tush was a bit tender for the next few days.

Do Dogs Go to Heaven?

When I was still in my pre-school years, we had a dog named Frisky. Frisky was completely black—a "Heinz 57". All our farm dogs were mixed, with a bit of one breed sometimes being more dominant, but no one cared about having purebred dogs. A good farm dog may have a bit of border collie in them, or not. To us, Frisky was just a black dog.

And then we acquired a puppy I named Charlie.

Charlie was also a Heinz 57. Frisky and Charlie were my playmates while Janice was at school and I was at home with my parents. Except for mealtimes, Dad was almost always outside working with the animals or farming, and Mom was often busy in the garden or cooking or baking, so when I wasn't following one of them around, I amused myself with my pets: teaching my dogs to play dead, sit, and fetch; exploring the farmyard and surrounding field with them; or just sitting with them on my lap petting them.

We had had both dogs for a couple of years, and I was in the bathroom when I heard my dad enter the house and start talking to my mom. When I heard what he was saying, I froze on the toilet.

"I found the dogs."

"Where were they?" Mom asked.

"Over in the Bill Willer place. Shot dead. Laying in the summer fallow."

Shot. Dead.

Who would shoot my dogs? I thought. I felt a rock form in my stomach.

My dogs are dead. Dead. Why would someone come onto our land and shoot our dogs?

"They were in *our* field?" my mom asked.

"Yup."

"I bet it was the Edmundsons. They would do something like that—come onto our land and shoot our dogs if they had been running around on their land instead of coming and talking to us."

"Guess so."

"Are you going to talk to them?"

"What for? The dogs are dead."

That word again.

Dead.

And then I had another terrifying thought.

My mom took me and my sister to Sunday school at the Evangelical church in Hanna. In a thirty-minute lesson each week, we were told that unless you "accept Jesus Christ as your

Lord and Savior and invite him to come and live in your heart," you are doomed to spend eternity in hell. And even when we were at that tender age, our teachers also told us that animals don't have souls and therefore do not go to heaven.

If Frisky and Charlie aren't going to be in heaven, I don't want to go there! I thought, as I continued to huddle in the small half-bathroom. *If they aren't in heaven, where are they? When I die, I want to go wherever they are now.*

I kept my butt on the toilet for what felt like hours to a six-year-old. As long as I stayed in the bathroom, I wouldn't have to face life without my dogs.

"Lorna, what are you doing in there for so long?" Mom called to me.

I pulled up my pants, flushed the toilet, and slowly opened the door. As I exited the bathroom, I looked up at my parents. My bottom lip was trembling, and as I briefly met my mom's gaze, the look on her face told me that she then realized I had heard them talking. I ran into my purple room, slammed the door, threw myself on my bed, and started wailing.

We never had a conversation about the dogs.

Vermin

Not long after we knew Frisky and Charlie were never coming back, the four of us were at a neighbour's house for an evening visit. They had some puppies that they needed to get rid of and so my parents made a business transaction: one puppy in exchange for a dozen eggs.

I immediately claimed this soft, brown-and white, floppy-eared, border collie-ish, Heinz 57 doggie as my own and named her Sally. It seemed like a great name to a six-year-old.

One of Sally's first tasks was to make an appearance in my grade one class for Show and Tell. I placed Sally in the ubiquitous cardboard box that all kids carted their pets and other creatures around in and Mom drove us to school. I proudly stood at the front of the room and displayed her to my classmates. Somehow, I managed to muster up a few words and proclaim in a few sentences, "This is my new dog. Her name is Sally." The end. That was the most my classmates heard me speak throughout all of grade one.

***

Our teachers were tolerant beings. Every now and then a student brought a new puppy or kitten to Show and Tell. But other times, some of us brought other critters. My other live contribution to Show and Tell came soon after I learned how to ride a bike.

Nut Bags and Num-Nums

I struggled to learn how to ride a bike. I had, and still have, terrible balance, so I was forever getting my dad to take the training wheels off my bike, sure I was ready *this time*, but then quicky realizing I was out of my league and getting him to put them back on. He and my mom started to get impatient with me, and he got tired of swapping my training wheels off and on, but as much as I wanted to be, I was never ready to graduate to two wheels.

Mom, Dad, and I were sitting at the dining room table in the afternoon when I decided to go outside and again try riding my bike. The training wheels were off.

The driveway had a slight slope to it. Without pedalling, I sat on the bike and coasted down the slope and onto the road. I lifted my feet off the ground and held them beside the pedals. I made it about a hundred feet—the farthest I had ever gone—before the bike slowed down and I fell over.

Wow! I actually rode my bike!

I ran into the house.

"Did you see that! I rode my bike all the way to the road without falling off!"

My mom replied, "Do it again, but when you slow down, start pedalling."

Oh yeah. Good idea.

I had been so excited about keeping my balance, I forgot about pedalling.

Nut Bags and Num-Nums

I ran back outside and coasted down the slope. This time, when my bike slowed, I pedalled for a few moments before I lost my balance and fell.

It didn't matter that I had fallen. I had gone farther than the first time.

I went back to the top of the driveway, started again, and pedalled a bit farther this time. Over and over until I could pedal down the road a short distance without losing my balance.

Once I had this newfound mode of transportation and starting biking down the road for fun, I began to encounter more wildlife, including snakes. I'm not terrified of snakes as some people are, but I don't like them. Whenever I saw a snake on the road and realized I was going to be riding over it, I lifted my legs. I knew they were all harmless garter snakes, usually only around twenty inches long or a bit more, but still, *you never know*. It would be just my luck to drive my bike over the one rabid, vicious, jumping garter snake on the whole continent and meet my demise.

I had, after all, seen *Jaws* and was wary of any creatures that I wasn't used to dealing with. We lived nowhere near the ocean, but the opening scene of the movie when the woman is swimming solo in the ocean and gets attacked by the shark permanently traumatized me. After I saw that scene, I was terrified of taking a bath.

What if a shark comes up from the drain and attacks me?

I kept my eye on that drain good and hard every time I took a bath.

Nut Bags and Num-Nums

I had been under strict instructions to go to bed the night my parents watched *Jaws* on TV but instead, I snuck out of my room and hid behind my dad's recliner until that opening scene scared me enough to send me back to my room. I'm not sure that my parents ever knew the reason behind my irrational fear of the bathtub drain.

In spite of my wariness of snakes, I was not deterred from having my dad pick up a garter snake that I found on the road, put it into an ice cream bucket, and send it with me on the school bus for Show and Tell. No cardboard box for this critter. The snake needed to be in an ice cream bucket so that the lid would ensure there were no jail breaks.

Greasy Grimy Gopher Guts

After her public appearance, Sally settled into life on the farm as an outdoor dog who was victim of a great deal of attention from her self-proclaimed owner. As soon as I got home from school, I rushed to play with her, often dressing her up in my doll's clothes or taking off out of the farmyard to explore the fields and pastures together.

Sally grew to be a loyal, dependable farm dog, accompanying us when we rode off on our horses for enjoyment or to check cattle. She chased cattle out of the farmyard when they wandered in from the pasture, and she was always up for rolling around on the ground with me. A committed gopher hunter, she loved chasing them in the field, catching them with her teeth, and shaking her head while they squeaked and shrieked.

Mom and Dad encouraged Janice and me to assist in controlling the gopher population on our land.

"Gophers are a nuisance. They eat the crops, and the holes they dig are dangerous. Cows and horses could trip in the holes and break a leg," Dad told us.

He took us to town to buy gopher traps, showed us how to use them, and set us loose, telling us to ... *gopher it.*

He didn't teach us what to do with the gophers once we trapped them; we figured that out ourselves.

Nut Bags and Num-Nums

I was always excited to check the traps because a catch meant extra money. In addition to our regular allowance, Mom paid us five cents for every gopher we caught until we got a little older and negotiated a raise to twenty-five cents. (When we told our neighbour about our successful business negotiation with our mom, his response was, "Boy, inflation sure hit the gopher market!")

One spot in our pasture was especially profitable. There was an entire mound that the gophers had built up over the years, and we could almost always see the little critters running around the mound, squeaking, chasing each other, playing. We pounded our stakes into the ground, secured the traps to the stake, set the trap in the hole, and left. We trekked back once or twice a day to see if we had caught anything.

"Let's go check the gopher traps!" was one of the main sentences I often uttered during the summers of my childhood. This was one adventure I sometimes took the lead on.

Janice, Sally, and I headed out to the mound, hammer and bailer twine in tow.

"There's a gopher in my trap! What do I do with it?" I asked Janice when I discovered my first catch.

"Bang it on the head with the hammer."

"Okay."

Tap.

"That didn't kill it," I told her.

"Hit it harder. Like this."

She took the hammer from me.

BAM!

The Bunny Foo Foo approach didn't work for me; I was too timid to smite the gopher hard enough with the hammer to snuff it out. Plus, I was scared the evil gophers, or the fleas they were surely infested with, would bite me and I'd be plagued with some incurable gopherific disease. The whole action felt so personal and vicious and scary.

"There has to be a better way," I told Janice. "What if we smash it with a rock?"

"Yeah, that'll work."

I picked up a rock and dropped it on the gopher from waist height.

SPLAT!

The guts and eyeballs squirting out from underneath the rock confirmed my success.

After that, I stuck with the rock method. It was more effective and less intimate.

We tied bailer twine around their necks or bellies and brought the whole critter back to show Mom so she would pay us. Knowing that Sally liked to play with the gophers, we sometimes tied the twine around them while they were still alive in the trap.

Nut Bags and Num-Nums

"Get 'im, Sally!"

When we heard the gopher's bones crunching between Sally's teeth as she bit down on them, we concluded, "Well that's one less gopher Dad needs to worry about." She never ate them but she loved to help annihilate them.

Why should Sally have all the fun? I thought.

I tied the rope around the gopher's neck or tummy and then swung the rope around in the air as if it were a lariat.

Every now and then, I failed to tie the twine tight enough.

FWIIINNNNNGGG!

The gopher went flying through the air, landing fifty feet away, and I lost my income.

When I didn't send the gopher flying, once it had had several trips on the invisible Tilt-A-Whirl, I let it back on the ground and watched it stagger around before bashing it with a rock or sic'ing Sally on it. When it was good and dead, I brought it home to collect my wages.

Pet or Food?

There's a bit of a grey area when it comes to some farm animals. Dogs and cats are definitely pets. Others, like snakes and skunks, are definitely not. Horses are pets but for us, they were also part of the workforce.

When it comes to cattle, pigs, chickens, and turkeys, what may start out as a pet often lands on the dinner plate.

I was always excited when my mom came home from town in the spring with the new baby chicks she had ordered from the United Farmers of Alberta (UFA). Boxes of chirping tennis-ball-sized yellow fuzzballs were on the back seat of her car, and Janice and I rushed to the chicken coop help her settle the chicks into their new home.

One by one, we picked up a baby chick, held it gently but also firmly enough that it wouldn't squirm away, dipped its beak into the water enough times until it learned how to drink (usually two or three), and then released the chick. Mom always got at least a hundred baby chicks, often more. She wanted to raise enough chickens for us to eat throughout the year, but she got extra so that both my sets of my grandparents could have some in their freezers, as well. She also used to sell some of the ready-to-eat chickens to townsfolk. There were no regulations requiring food products to be inspected. The townspeople were thrilled to have fresh farm chicken.

Nut Bags and Num-Nums

I was always sad to see the white feathers sprouting on the baby chickens and turkeys only a few days after they arrived on the farm. As they matured, they weren't nearly as cute.

Turkeys were the worst. They turned into stupid animals that sometimes needed to be reminded how to eat or drink. At night, when we shooed the turkeys and chickens back into their house, the turkeys ran hither and yon, with deer-in-headlights looks on their faces, gobbling and squawking as if the world were ending. And, I never witnessed this on our farm, but I often heard stories of turkeys drowning when they were outside in a rainstorm, heads turned upward, mouths open, watching the rain, because they swallowed enough water to drown.

But oh, the turkeys were delicious come Easter, Thanksgiving, and Christmas.

We butchered most of the chickens we raised about six weeks after we got them, but Mom also made sure we had enough laying hens to keep us and many others supplied with eggs. As the baby of the family, my job, as soon as I was old enough, was to go to the hen house to collect the eggs twice a day. I was always scared to stick my hand into the box where a hen was sitting for fear she would peck at me.

But I was excited to see how many eggs were in each nest. Although I complained about doing my chores, as every kid is required to do, I secretly looked forward to heading out to the chicken house to retrieve warm eggs that I knew would make a tasty breakfast or that Mom would use for baking.

I was particularly fascinated when I collected an egg that hadn't formed a shell. Once in a while, I reached into the nest and found a squishy egg, the yolk and white surrounded only by a thick membrane. It was as if the chicken had birthed a small, thick-skinned water balloon. These were real eggs, but they had to be handled gently so the membrane wouldn't burst. They were a weird texture, and finding one was always a fun surprise.

The one chicken-related chore I hated was cleaning out the coop. We used straw for bedding, and with the number of chickens in the house, the straw quickly got musty and caked with chicken shit. Ah, the smell of musty straw and chicken doo-doo on a hot summer day! We used grain shovels to clear everything out of the house onto the wagon so Dad could haul it away. We then spread a new batch of straw around the chicken house. It was dusty, heavy, stinky, hard work, and every time I finished, I immediately went into the house to have a bath and change clothes.

Every June, our weekends were booked up with butchering chickens and attending branding parties. My grandparents came out from town on Saturdays and we all got to work on the assembly line, taking live chickens through the process to become freezer- or frying pan-ready.

My parents assigned me and my sister the job of catching the chickens with the chicken catcher—a piece of hard wire about four feet long with a hook at the end. (The easiest way to make one of these is to straighten out a wire clothes hanger and form a hook at the end of it, but Dad always had lots of wire around the farm to use, too.) We had to be quick, sneaking up on each chicken, slowly pushing the catcher toward them and then quickly pulling back when we hooked the end around their leg.

There was a definite art to this; the chickens scared easily, so we had to be sneaky but also fast at the right moment.

As soon one of us caught a chicken, we took it to Dad, who chopped off its head and then let it flop around on the ground until it bled out. The idiom "running around like a chicken with its head cut off" is accurate. Once Dad had beheaded all of the chickens, we gathered them up from wherever they had flopped to—sometimes we had to crawl under the car to get them, sometimes we had to hunt elsewhere. Some of them travelled far in their final moments.

The next step was to dip them into steaming water to soften the skin and then pluck the feathers. The electric feather plucker was a machine that most farmers who raised chickens had: a round small, barrel-shaped wheel on a stand with rubber fingers. When plugged in, the wheel rotated quickly and sent the feathers flying when we pressed the chicken against it.

We needed to do a thorough once-over of each chicken by hand because the machine removed most of the feathers but not all of them. We still had to remove the tail, wing, and neck feathers manually. There were also always pinfeathers—the root of the feather—which needed to be pulled out, especially under the wings. We could got some out with our fingers, but we used strawberry hullers or anything resembling a large pair of tweezers for the obstinate ones.

Once the chickens were naked, we removed the innards.

My mother and grandmas taught me how to gut a chicken:

Nut Bags and Num-Nums

1. Make a small cut in the neck—just large enough to stick your fingers into.

2. From here, you should be able to feel and pull out the esophagus. (It feels and kind of looks like a bendy straw.) Pull it out as far as you can until you meet resistance, and then cut it off at the base. Throw it at your sister when your parents aren't looking.

3. Make a larger cut slightly below the breast bone, but not too deep; you don't want to cut into the inner organs.

4. Pull open the chicken at the bottom cut. The opening needs to be large enough to stick your hand into.

5. Insert your hand, keeping your fingers along the top of the cavity. Run your hand all the way back as far as you can, and then pull everything out by scooping. You may need to scoop and pull a few times, loosening the innards from the inside of the chicken's body. Once you have all of the innards on the table, you need to deal with them.

6. The gizzard is a round, hard organ with a blue fanned pattern on each side. Cut it away from the rest of the innards. Slice it in half, but don't cut all the way through. Slice only a centimeter deep or a bit more. Then, pull it open. Inside you will find a sac containing whatever the chicken last ate—probably the grain you fed them and a few small pebbles. If you pull the gizzard open enough, you can easily peel away the sac, which you will then discard. Your mother will fry the gizzard for dinner that night, and you and your older sister will fight over who gets to eat it because you both love it and there is only one.

Nut Bags and Num-Nums

(Sometimes your mom will cut it in half in order to get the two of you to stop fighting over it.)

7. Find the heart. It's roughly the size of a large grape and is easily identifiable. Cut it away from the rest of the organs, cutting off the valves. It too will be fried later. If you got to eat the heart last time, your sister will get it this time, and vice versa.

8. Find the liver. This, you need to be careful with. The liver is slippery and is attached to the body by the bile duct. You *do not* want to burst the bile duct. Get a good grasp on the liver with one hand, and cut just above the bile duct with your knife, separating the liver from the rest of the innards. Neither you nor your sister will eat the liver for dinner that night because you both pretend you don't like it.

9. Once you have retrieved these three organs, you can then discard the rest of the innards.

10. The inside of the chicken still needs some cleanup. Reach in and find the lungs. They are between the neck and the ribs. You should be able to scoop them out in one piece with your index and middle finger. Hopefully they remain intact; if not, getting them out will be a bit messy. If you mash them, they will easily come out when you rinse the inside of the chicken, but the goal is to peel them out in one piece. (These also make great slime bombs to throw at your sister when your parents aren't looking.)

11. Do the same for the kidneys, which are at the bottom of the body near the opening.

12. Once you have all of the organs out, plop the chicken into the tub of cold water and start on the next one.

The process is the same for turkeys; they are just much bigger.

***

Every June, we butchered those one hundred chickens (unless some had died). Dealing with all of them required working all day for several days.

After all the chickens had been butchered and packaged up for the year, my parents rewarded me and my sister with a banana split at the local drive-through. Any other time of the year, we might get a chocolate dipped soft ice cream cone as the odd treat, but the only time we each got our own banana split was as payment when chickens were done. Sometimes my parents took us to town for our treat within a few days or even in the evening of the last day of butchering, but many years, we had to wait several weeks or even a month or more if there were other demands on the farm in summer months.

"Don't you still owe us a banana split for butchering chickens?" my sister or I would ask Mom.

"Yes, I know. I haven't forgotten," she would assure us, and we would get our banana splits before the drive-in burger place shut down for the summer.

Years after Janice and I had left home and Mom stopped raising chickens, we still pushed our luck any time we were home for a visit.

Nut Bags and Num-Nums

"Don't you still owe us a banana split for butchering chickens?" we'd ask.

"Nice try." Mom would smirk.

***

My chicken butchering skills served me and my team well when I was in Peru for six weeks in the summer of 1988.

My biggest dream since I was eight was not only travelling but also working abroad. When I was eighteen and finishing my first year of university, the first opportunity for me to realize this dream arose.

One of my university friends told me of a non-denominational mission organization that sent teams of teens and young adults to various countries to volunteer for different projects. I applied and was accepted to go to Peru.

My team of twenty-six teenagers was led by four young adults in their early- to mid-twenties. Three of us were from Alberta, and the rest were from across Canada and the US. We were plopped in the middle of the Peruvian jungle, an eight-hour drive from Lima and ten miles from the closest town. Our camp had running water only in the kitchen; we showered and did laundry under the waterfall in the river, which was a ten-minute hike from the camp down into a valley.

We also had no electricity. At nighttime, after the sun set at 6:00pm, we entertained ourselves with light from lanterns and candles. We played checkers on a board made from a towel and used rocks as game pieces. Two of us had brought guitars with us and so groups of us spent a lot of time playing and singing together. Other team members had brought other small games and to play with.

Roughly halfway through our stay in this camp, one of the local farmers gifted our group with five chickens he had killed that day. They were plucked, but that was all. No one had a clue what to do with them, and we were eager to eat them because we'd been living for weeks on canned beef, canned beans, and powdered milk.

We were digging a trench by hand with shovels when one of our group leaders announced to us the arrival of these chickens and the ensuing dilemma.

I stuck up my hand and said, "Give me two or three people and I can get these ready for supper tonight."

And thus, in the middle of a South American jungle, I taught a couple of city kids how to get chickens ready for the frying pan. We enjoyed a great meal that night.

Nut Bags

My parents didn't have much cash on hand when I was growing up. Everything they earned went back into the farm: buying new machinery, buying more cattle or horses, buying a newer car or truck, fixing the old machinery, and acquiring more land. During the 1980s, when interest rates on loans were at 18 per cent, they struggled to make payments on their loans.

We kids didn't get many treats. But we knew we would get treats from Dad when he went to town to buy parts for machinery or to sell grain. He consistently brought us back chocolate goodies, usually Glossette raisins, Cherry Blossoms, or Whole Almonds chocolate bars.

The hamlet of Richdale is a few miles east of our farm along the highway. If Dad was going there to do business or if he was helping out a neighbour in that area, he always stopped at the general store on his way home and brought us each a Creamsicle, Revello, or Fudgesicle.

Dad did a lot of business at K & B Motors in Hanna, owned by Ken and Bruce. Ken and Bruce had one of those old chest vending machines that sold pop. When Janice and I were with Dad and he stopped at K & B, he gave us each a quarter so we could get bottle of grape or orange pop to keep us distracted while he visited with his buddies and did his business.

Nut Bags and Num-Nums

Pop was one treat we got a bit more often than others. In the summers, our family sometimes spent Sunday afternoons driving up and down the highway with us kids jumping out of the car or truck any time we saw a bottle in the ditch. We threw it in a bag, and once we had enough, we took the bottles back to the depot in town. With the money from the returns, my parents bought a case of pop from The Pop Shop.

We also made our own root beer. It was always tortuous to wait those several weeks until the root beer had fermented and was ready to drink. We usually bottled it in those stubby little brown bottles. I was quickly learning those bottles *always* had good stuff in them!

Every November, Bruce had another treat in store for us— one that was only available that time of year. Being heavily interested and invested in horses and rodeo, my family faithfully watched the National Rodeo Finals (NFR) on TV every year, and each year, Bruce, the local Hesston dealer, had a Hesston NFR belt buckle for me and my sister. Each year the buckles were different. These were pretty special collectors' items. Although we never got to travel to see the NFR in person, we cherished these buckles "from Bruce," as we called them.

I still have all of mine.

***

One guaranteed treat each December was what we called Uncle Emil's Nut Bags.

Uncle Emil and Grandpa (my mom's dad) were brothers. Uncle Emil's wife, my aunt Rosie, and my grandma were sisters.

Nut Bags and Num-Nums

So, two brothers married two sisters. For their entire adult lives, Grandma and Auntie Rosie talked to each other at least once a day on the phone. When they were on the farm as young women, they lived a mile up the road from one another and often helped each other with farm duties and raising their kids. When both couples retired and moved into Hanna, their houses were a couple of blocks from each other. Grandma and Rosie were the best of friends. I always thought of Emil and Rosie as though they were almost a third set of grandparents because they treated us so well and we saw them so often.

Every Halloween, Uncle Emil and Auntie Rosie had a special bag of goodies set aside for us at their house, complete with homemade treats such as popcorn balls, puffed wheat squares, or Rice Krispies squares.

Uncle Emil and Grandpa were both heavily involved in the church I grew up attending. My grandpa helped build the church along with other volunteers. Uncle Emil contributed tirelessly as a member helping organize events, including the annual Christmas concert. One of his main duties was to prepare the treat bags for the kids.

Every year, Janice and I performed in some sort of church play for Christmas. When we were little, it was the typical nativity scene and we were usually angels. Then, as we got older, our youth group leaders found scripts of Christmas-themed plays for us to put on. I have no idea what my acting skills were like; of course, according to people in the church who had known me all my life, I was the next Jane Fonda or Katherine Hepburn. I was always praised for my acting abilities, and as shy as I was, I enjoyed performing in front of an audience.

Nut Bags and Num-Nums

At the end of the night, every kid in the church got one of the treat bags Uncle Emil had put together. And every year, the contents were similar: hard candies, wrapped candies, a candy cane, a mandarin orange, and lots of nuts—peanuts, chestnuts, and walnuts, all in their shells. Of course, we kids loved the candy much more than the nuts, so we whined about the nuts and wished there was more chocolate instead of nuts. But we loved those treat bags. Janice and I even got two of Uncle Emil's "nut bags" if there were extras once everyone had gotten one.

I was in my early twenties and living in Japan when Auntie Rosie passed away. My main goal is to live life with no regrets. But the one regret I have is that I was too far away to be able to attend her funeral. After she died and the next time I was in Canada, I visited Uncle Emil. He guided me to the china cabinet and told me to pick something to remember Auntie Rosie by. I chose a china teacup and saucer with yellow roses on it. Roses to remember Rosie.

Several years later, when my uncle's health started to fail, I was back living in Alberta. It seemed evident that his time was drawing near, so I drove out to Hanna from Calgary so I could visit him in the hospital.

I sat on the chair. He was having none of that. He patted the bed beside him and told me to sit there. I obeyed.

As soon as I sat down, he took my tiny hand in his large hand, permanently rough, tanned, and weathered from years of farm work.

"You're still my Little Lorna," he said as he smiled at me and patted the hand he was holding.

He asked how my job was going, what was new in my life.

And then the dagger.

"Are you going to church?" he asked me.

"No," I told him honestly.

He lifted his other hand and shook his thick index finger at me.

"Go to church, young lady," he scolded me.

I didn't make him any promises.

When I left, I gave him a big hug and he patted my hand again, telling me to behave myself.

That was the last time I saw him.

The Nuts We Liked

Dad's calves were born in February through March, and by May and June, they were ready to be branded, tagged, and vaccinated.

Janice and I were expected to respond when a parent banged on our bedroom door at 2:00am because a cow was giving birth and needed help. Sometimes Dad could handle this task on his own, but other times, all four of us needed to be out there, directing a cow in distress from the corral into the barn, where Dad tied her up and proceeded to help her. The cow, of course, didn't understand that we were there to help her, and sometimes we needed to be quick and agile to avoid getting kicked or charged by an angry, scared bovine.

Often, we were in the barn for an hour or two in the middle of the night. (In reality, this situation could happen anytime day or night but for some reason, the cows seemed to most often want to get us out of our warm beds in the middle of a cold winter night.) My and my sister's main jobs, because we were too young and not strong enough to handle the cow, would be to open and close gates, fetch hot water and disinfectant, hold towels, and do other supporting tasks.

I watched as my dad disinfected his arms, reached inside the cow sometimes all the way up to his shoulder, and helped guide the newborn calf to the outside world.

Nut Bags and Num-Nums

It was always such a relief to see a slimly baby calf emerge from the cow's behind and start to struggle to stand. Once the calf was on its feet and getting its first taste of milk, we were allowed to go back to bed.

Inevitably, some of the calves didn't survive. And there were times when the calf survived but its mother didn't. These were the calves I fell most in love with, and I was able to help more with them. Dad kept them in the barn and tasked me and Janice with feeding them. Their food consisted of a powder that we mixed with water. We fed the calves from pails with a rubber nipple protruding from near the bottom.

The calves soon learned that we were not only friendly, but we were the source of their warm, delicious food, and after the first few meetings, they ran toward us, thrust their mouths around the nipple, and ate. While they enjoyed their nourishment, we scratched their heads and admired their beautiful eyes and eyelashes.

It was because of this part of my childhood that I could relate to Fern in *Charlotte's Web*—a book that became one of my favourites the first time I read it. And I read it countless times. Every time I finished the book, I immediately started reading it again and again. It was only when I was in my late forties and moving to a new house and therefore trying to downsize a bit that I got rid of my childhood copy of *Charlotte's Web*, which had long since become a stack of single pages.

***

In May and June, cattle ranchers hosted a branding. We made our rounds to each ranch, helping out. Each person attending had their own role to play. One of my favourite roles, from the time I could ride a horse on my own, was to join the roundup of the cattle. At sunrise, several ranchers and their kids and/or wives took their horses to the home of whoever was hosting the branding and headed out to the pasture to help bring the cattle in. Once the cattle were penned, the cows were separated from the calves for the day, and when the rest of the helpers arrived, the branding began.

Two of the men roped the calves and brought them close to the propane-powered fire pit in which the branding irons were kept hot. A couple of the men did the branding, and a couple more did the castrating. My dad was one of the designated castrators. Vaccinating the calves fell to a couple of other men, one or two of the women if there were some out in the corral helping, or one or two of the teenagers.

The other teenagers were in charge of "wrastling"—holding the calves down on the ground—one at the head and one at the heel. The header squatted down with one knee on the ground and the other on the calf's neck, placing just enough pressure to keep it from jumping up. The header also secured the calf's top leg, curled back and held tight so the calf couldn't get up. The heeler was on the back end, butt on the ground, legs stretched out. One leg was behind the calf and the other would be just under the calf's butt, pushing the bottom leg away so that it couldn't kick back. The heeler held and pulled back on the calf's other back leg. The two wrastlers held the calf while it was branded, vaccinated, and castrated (if it were male). Ear tags were put on one ear as an additional marking to show who they belonged to.

Nut Bags and Num-Nums

Each rancher had a brand registered with the government. My dad's brand was on the left rib of the animal. Other ranchers' brands may have been on the right side and some were on the hip rather than the rib or belly. Thus, it was important that the calves were laying on the proper side so they were branded on the correct hip or side of the belly.

Another important job was assigned to one of the younger children—a kid or two who were old enough to walk and carry a bucket but not old and strong enough to wrestle the calves. The nut pail was usually a one-gallon plastic ice cream bucket that the kid or kids carried around, following the men who were doing the castrating. The Master Castrators placed the testicles in the bucket after ripping them out of the poor calves' nether regions.

Once the work in the branding corral was finished, the next task for the children and teenagers was to clean the testicles. We were all taught the proper way to clean a calf nut: Hold it in one hand and pull on the membrane on the outside so that it was good and tight around the testicle. Then, slice the membrane—but not too deeply—so that it could be peeled away and removed, revealing the testicle itself. At some point during the cleaning, the teenage boys made sure they threw a few of the slimy nuts at the younger kids (especially the girls), prompting the little ones to run away screaming in fake terror.

Once the testicles were all skinned, someone took them into the house, where the women washed them, dipped them into a bowl containing a beaten egg, and dipped them into another bowl coating them in bread crumbs or crushed crackers. The women then fried the prairie oysters until they were cooked all the way through. Prairie oysters were the treasured appetizers after a long day of work on what was often a hot, dry day.

"Tastes like chicken"? Nah. More like ... veal.

The day ended with a big meal. The wife of the rancher hosting the branding spent the day in the house cooking and also did some cooking and baking in the days leading up to the branding. We knew we'd get certain foods at each farm. One of our neighbours always had a rich, creamy, chocolate Skor bar cake for dessert. Mom's expected dessert every year was her ice cream pie—a frozen dessert with a chocolate crumb crust, a layer of vanilla ice cream topped with a layer of chocolate sauce, then a layer of whipped cream. The whipped cream layer was garnished with more chocolate cookie crumbs and maraschino cherries. (Both my mom and dad's side of the family also expected the ice cream pie at every holiday meal.) The main meal at every ranch was assuredly always beef—burgers or roast beef. One of our neighbours also served deep fried turkey.

There was seemingly unlimited chilled beer and pop in coolers and big tubs that were partially filled with ice. Lawn chairs and other chairs were set up in the garage or in the yard so that all workers could relax and enjoy a huge, home-cooked meal after their hard work. Sometimes, there might be a ball game in the pasture later or a game of horseshoes.

Although I was a girl, I considered it a badge of honour once I got old and strong enough to be one of the wrastlers. I was a tomboy, so making it to this level was a source of pride for me knowing I could keep up with the neighbour boys. Mom would have definitely preferred having me in the house helping her with the cooking all day, but I always found an excuse to be outside, finding a job for myself and making sure I was needed in the corral.

The brandings were a practical event gathering lots of people to share in the work that needed to be done, but they also served as great social gatherings—a chance for neighbours to help one another and then have a great meal and fun evening together.

The Chuckshot Show

Janice started school when I was learning how to walk, so I spent almost all of my time in the first five years of my life with my mom and dad, a pet or two, and the TV. My days were carefree and fun, helping my mom make buns or cookies, wandering around the farm with my dad or a dog, watching *Sesame Street* and my other favourite shows: *Mr. Dressup*, *Romper Room*, and *The Polka Dot Door*, all of which were on in the morning.

My kindergarten class was half days every morning thus permanently robbing me of all of my favourite TV shows once I started attending school. I was devastated to not be able to watch my favourite shows any more. Add to the mix that I was terrified of spending all morning five days a week with kids I didn't know. The first day my mom dropped me off at the elementary school, I stood outside the big red doors and sobbed, desperately wanting her to come back and take me home. After I had been wailing for a few minutes, a teacher took me inside to the kindergarten classroom.

After that day, I rode the bus in the mornings and when kindergarten was over at noon, I either went to my grandma's house or looked for my mom to pick me up from the school.

There was a bit of hierarchy on the bus. The older kids got to sit at the back, so the younger you were, the closer your seat was to the front. Since I was the baby of the group I was in the front seat. Most of us kids on the bus knew each other because

Nut Bags and Num-Nums

our parents were neighbours and helped each other when cattle escaped from pastures and needed to be rounded up or when extra hands were needed during brandings and harvest.

I have large, deep blue eyes, and being the shy, weird, socially inept kid that I was, I often silently stared at people. Twin boys from a neighbouring farm were on my bus, and they were two years older than me. One of them nicknamed me Frog Eyes, and while part of me liked the attention, I hated the name. I sat on the bus seat in front of him and often turned around to stare at him and others. His acknowledgement of me and teasing with the nickname prompted me to turn around and face the front, thus isolating myself from the other kids talking to each other.

One of the TV shows I was no longer able to watch was a local kids' show produced in Calgary. *The Buckshot Show* was on every weekday at noon and on Saturday mornings. It featured Ron Barge, a local Calgary man ("Buckshot") wearing a goofy cowboy hat, singing and playing his guitar, and interacting with his puppet friends on the show: Clyde the Owl and Benny the Bear (B. T. Bear). On Saturdays, he had a small group of kids come into the studio, and the kids sat on a carpet while Buckshot talked and sang songs with his puppet friends. He called some of the kids up to interview them, asking who they were, asking where they were from, and having them tell him something about themselves.

The twin boys had an older brother, Chuck, who also rode the school bus. Once Chuck had made his way through the ranks and earned the back seat on the bus, he introduced The Chuckshot Show to our bus rides in the mornings. There were

Nut Bags and Num-Nums

no puppets, but kids sauntered from the front of the bus to the back to sit on Chuck's lap and be interviewed for his TV show.

The part of riding the school bus that I disliked the most was getting stuck waiting for trains. The route between our farm and the school crossed two train tracks. By law, the bus had to stop while the driver looked for trains. We almost never had to wait for a train at the train crossing on the highway. At the train tracks on the edge of town, however, we had to wait sometimes. The train schedule coincided with our passage to school, and on days when we arrived at the tracks at just the wrong moment, the bus driver had to wait sometimes for up to ten minutes while the train passed or partially passed and then backed up in order to switch tracks.

One of the younger boys on the bus threw up on the floor in the aisle in the middle of the bus. That morning, we got stuck waiting for the train. By the time it had passed, we had been enduring the smell of his barf for a good ten minutes. One of the cattle auction markets was on the other side of the tracks. By the time the bus was resuming its trek into town, we had had all of the windows open for several minutes already. The smell had dissipated only a bit, and as we passed the auction market, one of the twin boys stuck his head out the window declaring, "Even the stockyards smell good this morning!"

My first bus driver was a woman who lived on a farm a few miles west of my parents' place. She was a pleasant, gentle, kind woman with a melodious voice who was always gracious and patient with the kids on the bus.

"I don't feel very good," I told her one morning as she neared the elementary school. I was sitting in the front seat.

Nut Bags and Num-Nums

"What's the matter, Lorna?" she asked me. "Tummy not feeling right?"

"Yeah, I guess."

I slumped down in my seat, pouring it on a little harder.

"Do you feel good enough to go to school?"

"No, I don't think so. I think I want to go home."

Of course she couldn't take me home.

"Why don't I take you to your grandma's house and you can rest there until your mom comes to get you?"

"Okay."

The driver completed her route, dropping all the kids off at the elementary, junior, and then senior high school. I stayed on the bus. She then drove to my grandma's house, where she accompanied me to the door and explained the situation to my grandma. I spent the morning with my grandma, listening to her Anne Murray records. When my mom came to get me, I was met with skepticism.

"I don't think you are really sick," my mom said.

My stomach had been a bit flippy floppy. I wasn't so sick that I was bedridden, but I didn't feel up to going to school that day. In hindsight, it was likely my anxiety working itself up a bit. Maybe I just didn't have it in me to be around other kids that day, what with my great need for personal space and alone time. I went back to school the next day.

Nut Bags and Num-Nums

We had the same driver for a few years until she quit. Our next driver was a man who had recently moved to the area. He drove bus for a few years. He too was patient and kind. By the time he was our driver, I was in upper elementary school and was coming out of my shell a bit, so I always responded to his pleasant good morning greetings. Whenever I or another girl wore a dress to school, he complimented us, telling us, "You look absolutely...." He purposely left the sentence dangling so we would have to finish it with our imaginations.

My last bus driver was Auntie Barb. She wasn't my aunt. Her two daughters and her nephew also rode the bus. The nephew always called her Auntie Barb, so the rest of us started doing so as well. She seemed tickled that we did. When I got to be a teenager, Auntie Barb started a new club at her house for us kids to have something to do on a Thursday night. She hosted dance lessons for any of the neighbour kids who wanted to come. It wasn't really about the lessons; we had all grown up attending dances in the local community hall with our parents so we all knew how to dance. It was more of a chance for the teenagers on the farms in the area to get together for an evening to do something fun and safe. She charged us $5 a week, but the money all went into a jar, and when there was enough, she used it to buy pizza so we could have a pizza party in addition to our dance lessons.

The Unwanted Christmas Present

I was eight years old when I decided I wanted to become a teacher and teach in another country for a few years. I loved school, even throughout high school and university. When I was a student and especially after I became I teacher, I often reflected on what my teachers were doing to inspire and encourage their students. And I grumbled inwardly when I found their teaching methods uninspiring.

When I was teaching, I also looked back the times when I was confused, frustrated, and self-conscious as a student. This reflection helped me to be more aware of the students in my classes who often got overlooked, were too shy to speak up, or were struggling for any number of reasons. I'd like to think that I developed a higher sense of awareness and a greater sense of compassion by analyzing what worked for me as a student and what didn't.

One day in upper elementary school a couple of the boys threw spitballs while our teacher's back was turned. No one would tell the teacher who shot the spitballs against the blackboard even though we all saw it happen, so the teacher punished the whole class and kept us all in at recess. Punishing the whole class when the culprit was unnamed was typical for any infraction; every teacher employed this type of discipline, but I was always resentful of being lumped in and punished for something I didn't do. These incidents didn't diminish my respect for my teachers but I always felt it was unfair to punish

Nut Bags and Num-Nums

the blameless kids for what other kids were doing. I tucked all of this in the back of my mind and resolved that when I was a teacher, I would never punish a student for something someone else did.

With my shyness and reluctance to do *anything* lest it be wrong, I surprised myself when I gave in to peer pressure the day before Christmas vacation in grade one. We were supposed to go outside to play after finishing our lunch, but two of my classmates had the great idea that, as a Christmas present, they would clean up the teacher's desk before going outside. Somehow, I got tangled up in this plan. They asked me, and of course I didn't have the gumption to say no to anyone at that stage in life. We reorganized our teacher's desk, stacking books and papers neatly on top of one another and into piles. We placed some items into drawers and left for the playground feeling like we had been helpful. Her desk was certainly more organized than she had left it.

When we came back inside after lunch break was over, I was shocked and terrified to find that I was being summoned to the principal's office. The principal's office! This was where the bad kids were sent, and I was far from being one of those.

I don't know what I did wrong, but the kids that get called to the principal's office usually get the strap. Am I going to get the strap? Only the really bad kids get the strap.

The principal, a strict woman, separated the three of us who had tidied our teacher's desk. I was interrogated alone.

"Why did you move all of the things on your teacher's desk?" was her first question.

What was the right answer? The truth, obviously, but I was overshadowed by my confusion about why I was called to the principal's office for doing something nice for my teacher.

"Whose idea was it to organize your teacher's desk?" She tried a different approach—the "one of them will flip" tactic.

"Michelle," I squeaked out.

"And why did you take part?"

I was squirming on the chair, trying to muster up the courage to defend myself.

"We were just trying to help."

"What do you mean, 'help'? You are to never touch your teacher's desk or the things on it. Don't you know that?"

I hadn't known that. I didn't remember ever being told to never touch the teacher's desk. At home, I had chores to do; cleaning was one of those chores.

"I didn't know," I mumbled.

I was slinking down in my chair, my gaze fixed to the ground.

"Why did you move the things on your teacher's desk?" she tried again.

"We wanted to help. We thought that cleaning her desk would be a nice thing to do for our teacher for Christmas."

The principal paused.

Nut Bags and Num-Nums

"You are never to touch the things on your teacher's desk again. Do you understand?"

"Yes."

With that, she excused me and I went back to class.

So that's what we did wrong. We touched and moved our teacher's belongings.

But we didn't steal anything. We didn't damage or destroy anything. And our intentions were only good and kind. I was still confused.

I left school that day filled with fear. What else would I get in trouble for in the future if I didn't know what was allowed and what wasn't?

I was only six, but I recognized that my actions weren't perceived in the way they were intended. Our teacher obviously felt that we had intruded.

I was relieved that day as I walked out of the principal's office. Just the fact that I was called to the office meant, in my mind, I was going to get the strap. Having escaped with no physical punishment and only a scolding was a relief, and even at that young age, I recognized that the principal acknowledged my position and took mercy on me. She knew I wasn't a bad kid.

Boobies

My grade four teacher was a bit different than the other teachers I'd had up to that point in that she was a Miss, not a Mrs. We knew that meant that—gasp—she was a "spinster!" It was around that time that I started reading all of the books in the *Anne of Green Gables* series, and the marital status of my female teachers, in comparison to Anne, was a bit of a curiosity. I knew that in earlier times women commonly taught school until they were married, and I started to reflect on the fact that perhaps I was going to school at a time when this was shifting. Most of my female teachers were married, and we also had a couple of male teachers in our elementary school. Times had changed since the days of Anne.

I loved Miss Laverty. She was firm but kind and fair—encouraging without wavering in her control of the class. I was a people pleaser, and she motivated me to work hard by praising me when I completed my work early and with perfection.

It was during grade four, when I was in Ms. Laverty's class and when I was falling in love with Anne and the other characters in those books, that I decided I wanted to be a teacher. I wanted to be like Miss Laverty and Anne; I wanted to help students learn, and I wanted to inspire people. I was also devouring any books I could get my hands on and starting to experiment with doing my own creative writing.

Nut Bags and Num-Nums

Several months into the school year, I showed up with a single sheet of paper on which I had written. The subject of the poem was my dog, Sally, who I declared as my best friend. I showed the poem to Miss Laverty.

"What a wonderful poem! Sally sounds like a lovely dog."

As I was walking back to my seat with my poem in hand and pride in my heart, I heard one of my classmates whisper "teacher's pet" but I didn't care. I had written a poem, and my teacher thought it was good. I was going to be a teacher, but I was also going to be a writer, like Anne.

Grade four was also the year I started to learn about sex and about my own body. Neither of my parents ever had a conversation with me about sex; I learned from my classmates how babies are made. And a couple of the boys in my class told the rest of us about seeing magazines in their house called *Playboy* and *Penthouse*.

"Those magazines are full of pictures of naked ladies! You can see their boobies and everything!" they told us.

Miss Laverty often sent a couple of us to retrieve books for our lessons from the shelves at the back of her room. It didn't take one of our classmates long to discover the shelf of *National Geographic* magazines.

"Hey, look at this!" one of the boys pointed to a picture of a topless woman with dark skin and colourful necklaces on the cover. "It's like the magazines my dad has at home!"

Nut Bags and Num-Nums

After this discovery, some of us who went to the back of the room to get books took our time leafing through the pages of *National Geographic*. Any time Miss Laverty left the room, or if we were in the classroom at recess or lunch time without supervision, we ran straight to these magazines, flipping through them to find the pictures of women from different cultures who were baring their boobies. We thought it was so scandalous that a grade four teacher would have such magazines in her classroom.

Why does our teacher have these kinds of magazines in the back of our classroom? I wondered.

I quickly began to learn through leafing through the entire magazine, not just the booby pictures, that different cultures had different values, expectations, customs, and attire.

Being half or even fully naked in public in some cultures is normal. And the clothes they wear are so different from ours.

My curiosity about the world piqued and I longed to travel to see some of these people and places that were on those glossy pages. I wondered why it was okay to be naked in their culture but not in mine.

The pictures of the naked women only increased my curiosity of changes happening with my body. At first I thought I was just gaining weight (well, there was that, too). But when the actual shape of my body started to change and I noticed that my "raisins" (the word my mom used to refer to my nipples when I was little) and the skin around them were getting puffy, I realized I was entering a new phase—that my childhood was in the rear-view mirror. I was one of the first girls in my class to need a bra, and I started to feel self-conscious about my body. If I wore a bra, my classmates noticed it through my clothes, but if I didn't, my swollen raisins poked at my shirt from within. I wanted to reverse this change.

One of my classmates, Donald, played a bit of a role in bridging me from childhood to adolescence in a couple of minor ways. Up to that point, we boys and girls and all played together and I had given no thought to the differences between us. The only exception was in grade one when one of the boys in my class shared his cookies with me during recess. I remember feeling special and feeling liked.

Does this mean he wants me to be his girlfriend? I wondered.

But after I ate the cookie, nothing changed. He was simply being nice and sharing with me.

Donald, however, took things to a slightly higher level in grade four.

When Miss Laverty was out of the room and Donald and I were in the back of the room putting away textbooks, he suggested his idea.

"You hide back behind the bookshelves, and I'll go over there." He pointed to an area in the back of the classroom that was in view of everyone in the room. The area behind the bookshelves was not.

"And then when Miss Laverty comes back, I'll do this."

Nut Bags and Num-Nums

He turned around so his back was facing me, hugged himself so that his hands were on his shoulders, and started moving his upper body and head as if he were kissing someone.

"When she comes back, she'll think you and I are making out in the back of the room!"

I don't know why I agreed to this except that Donald could sell snow to polar bears and it was a silly idea. By grade four, I was trying to force myself to be less reclusive and I also liked practical jokes. I thought his idea was funny, and I wanted to see how Miss Laverty would react.

One of our classmates peeked out the door and when they saw her, hissed back at us, "She's coming!"

I took my place, hiding behind the bookshelf so no one could see me, and Donald went into action.

"Donald, quit being silly and take your seat," was all she said after glancing at him. She didn't mention me, and I came out from behind the bookshelf and went back to my desk.

My other coming-of-age memory involving Donald was small but it meant something big at the time. I came to school one day wearing a dress, and he commented, "Look at Lorna. She's trying to look pretty today!" I knew he meant it as a backhanded compliment, but I was on the verge of puberty when I was starting to become aware of my appearance and how boys perceived me. I *was* trying to look pretty that day, and even though I knew with 100 per cent certainty that Donald was teasing me and did not mean his comment to be hurtful, it was. It was months before I wore a dress to school again.

Premature Baldness

As much as I loved Miss Laverty and my grade four year, I hated grade five. Our grade five teacher was new to the school, new to town, and new to teaching.

Even as a nine-year-old, I could see that she was inexperienced, insecure, and disorganized. My classmates and I dreaded class each day. We were miserable. And our parents weren't happy, either.

"She isn't teaching our kids anything," my mom said. "I don't know what we can do, but something has to change."

My parents and I were at my friend Kelly's house halfway through the school year. My mom was talking to her mom while our dads were outside working with the horses. Kelly, her brother, and I were playing Monopoly in the living room and could overhear the conversation taking place in the kitchen.

"I called the principal again the other day and asked what they were doing about this," Kelly's mom said. She puffed on her cigarette. "He told me they were 'looking into it' but that doesn't help. They need to get off their asses and get rid of her now! This is bullshit!" Puff, puff, puff. "The whole year is just a goddam waste of time for these kids."

"Would they do that? In the middle of the school year?" Mom asked her.

"They goddamn better! I'll be making their lives a living hell until they do!" More puffing. "You want more coffee, Della?"

We were taught to respect our teachers, not talk back to them. And if we got in trouble at school, our parents always concluded that we were being rotten and deserved to be punished. But in this situation I saw, for the first time, that sometimes kids are right and the teacher is not. When the good kids were complaining that they weren't learning anything and that their teacher was unable to control the class or deliver a coherent lesson, the parents started to push back.

As the school year went on, students and parents became increasingly frustrated. We kids didn't understand a lot of what she was trying to teach us or what she said.

"Class, when you are sick with a sore throat, the best cure is to shine a UV light down your throat. That will kill the germs."

What? Really?

"Class, assemble," she said to us as we lined up to get on the bus for field trips or to leave our classroom for recess.

Assemble?

"Class, disperse," she told us when she dismissed us.

Disperse?

Maybe she is too smart for us. She doesn't know how to speak to grade five kids. Maybe she should be teaching at a college or university.

But one incident blasted that theory to smithereens.

Nut Bags and Num-Nums

"Class," she told us during Science, "in 1971 man first walked on the moon. This was a monumental moment in the history of space exploration."

"It was 1969," one of my classmates corrected her.

"ARE YOU TALKING BACK TO ME? ARE YOU?"

We all looked at her and froze. She had a habit of going from zero to full-on freak-out with no notice, but we were always stunned when it happened.

"But the moon landing was in 1969. You said it was 1971," the boy said.

"DON'T YOU TALK BACK TO ME!" She continued screaming.

"But you are wrong," he persisted.

He got up, went to the back of the room, picked up a book, and brought it back.

"See, it's right here."

He opened the book and pointed at one of the pages.

"DON'T YOU TELL ME I'M WRONG! I'M YOUR TEACHER."

"But you *are* wrong," he continued.

Oh oh..., I thought. *This is only going to get worse.*

Nut Bags and Num-Nums

The rest of us were still frozen, eyes darting back and forth between the two of them and each other. No one else dared move much less say anything.

She was at her desk, and he was about fifteen feet away at his desk in the middle row.

She started walking toward him, and he began backing away from her.

"DON'T YOU MOVE! DO YOU HEAR ME?"

You're screaming, lady. We can all hear you!

She started walking faster. He threw the book on the ground and ran away from her. She started running, too.

"DON'T YOU RUN AWAY FROM ME!"

Oh no. She's really lost it this time. She's going to murder him if she catches him.

My classmate scuttled up and down the rows, our teacher chasing him for several seconds until she caught up to him and seized a handful of hair on the back of his head.

"DO YOU WANNA BE BALD BEFORE YOU'RE FIFTY? DO YOU? DO YOU?" she screamed as she yanked repeatedly on his blonde hair. His head was jerking back and forth, and I could see the tears welling up in his eyes.

"DON'T YOU EVER TALK BACK TO ME AGAIN. DO YOU UNDERSTAND ME?"

What is going on? Why is she being so mean to him?

My classmates and I watched in shock and horror as she finally let go of his hair.

"Go back to your seat," she told him. He sat down and we all remained silent for the rest of the class.

***

My classmates and I had all but resigned ourselves to writing off our grade five year when, one day in May, our teacher was summoned to the principal's office in the middle of a lesson.

"Class, while I'm gone, read the rest of this chapter in your textbook and answer the questions on the board."

She left and we got to work.

I don't know how long she was gone. It felt like a long time. We were starting to wonder if she was ever coming back, when she finally entered the room crying.

"Class, I've been fired," she sobbed.

"HOORAY!" one of my classmates shouted. It was all I could do to stifle my laughter.

I lowered my head and eyes. A wave of relief immediately washed over me.

Maybe the rest of the school year will finally be enjoyable again, I thought. *I don't know who our new teacher will be but they can't be worse than this.*

As relieved as I was, I also felt sorry for her for being fired and so close to the end of the school year.

What is going on with her? I wondered. *Why was she such a bad teacher? What will she do for a job now? I wonder if she will teach somewhere else. But she got fired. Does that mean she won't be able to get a job in any other school? What will she do?*

The day she was fired was the last time we saw her. For the last six weeks of the school year we had a sub who was, by comparison, so "normal" that she was unmemorable.

Chicken Salad Sandwich

Music was one of my favourite classes in elementary school until grade six. For some reason, the powers that be who were in charge of writing Alberta curriculum thought that grade six students would love to learn the biographies of famous composers and, instead of playing instruments and learning how to read and play music, would be thrilled about spending all of Music class taking notes on this fascinating historical information. Every day we arrived in Music class to see the chalkboards filled with our teacher's handwritten notes on the life of the composer of the day.

We were required to sit quietly, copy the notes into our notebooks, and then hand them in for our teacher to review. If there was time remaining after the last kid had handed in their notebook, we could then play instruments.

After two weeks, I had had enough of that nonsense. I loved music, and our teacher, Mrs. Mohl, was a skilled pianist who always got us doing lots of singing and playing in class. I didn't understand why Music class in grade six had to become a read-and-take-notes dullfest.

***

The most rebellious I had been in school up to that point, other than the Christmas gift to my first grade teacher when we cleaned her desk, was in kindergarten when I was guilty of two misdemeanors. One was my refusal to answer the role call in school with "present" when my teachers called my name. My other form of rebellion was that I refused to drink the milk every day during milk and cookie time. I was a farm kid, raised on cow's milk. I didn't like the taste of store-bought milk. I don't recall getting into trouble for not drinking it, but I always felt I was being a bad kid for not drinking the milk.

At home, when my sister and I were fighting or not following orders, we got yelled at.

"Cut it out, you girls!" Mom often hollered at us.

Most of the time, when we were small-bad, a verbal reprimand was enough to get us to stop bickering.

When it wasn't though—when we were medium-bad—we got spanked. My mom's tools of the trade varied depending on what was within reach: fly swatter, wooden spoon, spatula, rubber spatula, whatever was handy and useful for the task.

"Janice and Lorna! I told you to knock it off!"

SMACK.

"You need to learn to play together without fighting."

WHACK.

We yowled as she wacked our asses, and then we went to our rooms to cry or pout.

Nut Bags and Num-Nums

I still remember going to school wearing shorts when I had welts in the pattern of the fly swatter showing on my legs at times.

"What's that neat design on your leg, Lorna?" one of my classmates asked me.

"Um, my mom spanked me with the fly swatter last night. Those bumpy circles are from the fly swatter."

Yeah, getting whacked with that thing wasn't neat. It HURT!

When my mom broke a wooden spoon in half because she wacked my butt so hard, I wanted to laugh. I knew though that laughing at her would heighten the situation to *large-bad*.

If we were *large-bad*—if we broke stuff, if we mouthed back to Mom, if we refused to do our chores, or if we didn't stop fighting—we had to wait until Dad got into the house.

"LORNA MARIE-AH! [emphasis on -AH] COME HERE!"

My middle name is Marie, but I knew when Mom turned it into Maria (Marie-AH!) I was in serious trouble. After Mom told Dad of our sins, he took his belt to our backsides. That was the ultimate discipline and the ultimate pain. When the lickin' was done, we ran to our rooms and cried it off.

"I was maybe five or six and I had reached an impasse with Dad about goodness knows what," Janice remembers. "I packed up a small blue-and-white hard shell suitcase full of toys and I set off walking down the road. I was done. I was running away from home. I think I got about three-quarters of a mile down the road when I heard Dad pull up the truck behind me. I was in trouble. I got the belt for that one. I didn't try to run away from home again."

It was the 1970s. Smacking kids was typical discipline. I grew up somewhat fearful of my dad, but I also knew that he wasn't to be feared unless I deserved a good hard wallop on the butt.

***

The fear of getting into trouble was no deterrent for me in grade six Music class, however. I was bored. Music was a huge love of mine outside of school and I was annoyed and felt robbed that we weren't getting to play in Music class. I revolted in a big way.

She doesn't read our notes anyway, I convinced myself after the first two weeks.

On the day of my sin, the composer of choice was Johann Sebastian Bach. How's this for foreshadowing: I really only learned the *actual* details of his life a couple of decades later when I visited some of the sites in Leipzig, Germany, where he lived and worked for several years until he died.

On Bach day in Music class, I dutifully opened up my notebook, took up my pencil, and began to write. Yes, write. *Not* copy notes from the chalkboard. I looked up at the board now and then to make it look like I was copying the notes, but I wrote, and I wrote feverishly. It flowed out of me without hesitation. A completely original, gripping, and entirely inaccurate story of Bach's life. As I wrote, I relaxed and actually enjoyed Music class for the first time in a couple of weeks, combining my love of music and writing.

Nut Bags and Num-Nums

When my classmates started handing in their notebooks, I quickly wrapped up my story, slapped my notebook shut, went up to the front of the classroom, and added my notebook to the pile. I was usually one of the first students finished my work in all of our classes, so I didn't want to take too long for fear that doing so would look suspicious.

She doesn't read our notes anyway, I reminded myself.

The end.

Until next Music class.

Mrs. Mohl always handed back our notebooks at the beginning of class so that we could use them to write that day's notes. She handed back everyone's notebooks ... except mine.

Uh oh.

"It seems that one of you decided to not follow instructions last class and instead of writing the notes from the board, wrote their own story," she announced as she gripped my notebook. She was glaring at me over her reading glasses.

Uh ... oh ...

I stared at my notebook in her hand.

I'm in big trouble.

I started squirming on my chair and slithering downward.

"This is what Lorna wrote in her notebook."

Nut Bags and Num-Nums

She opened my notebook and read aloud every word I had written, glancing up at me now and then above those damn reading glasses.

I was mortified. I desperately wanted aliens to swoop in through the window and abduct me. I kept glancing between the floor and the window. No UFOs. Nothing but blue sky. No hole in the floor for me to drop into, either. There was no escape.

As she continued, I heard some of my classmates snickering and giggling quietly off and on during parts of my story. I was so embarrassed and felt so ashamed, yet, part of me was a little proud that at least some of my peers thought this was funny and therefore were "on my side."

She slowed down, succinctly and loudly enunciating every word as she reached the end of the story:

"And ... he ... died ... at ... the ... age ... of ...eighty-four ... while ... eating ... a ... chicken ... salad ... sandwich."

She slapped my notebook shut.

Several of my classmates broke out into full-blown laughter.

I wanted to die. But I couldn't help but smirk a little, proud of my creativity. I thought it was a brilliant and dramatic ending to a famous life.

My teacher wasn't any more amused than she had been when she started to read my story.

She launched into a rant about following directions and behaving and punishment and blah blah blah wah wah wah—

she became Charlie Brown's teacher in front of the room. I tuned her out until I heard, "And do you want me to tell your parents about this?"

Without hesitation, I eked out, "No, I'll tell them."

I had no intention of telling my parents. This one was surely belt-worthy.

It seems she never did tell my parents. I certainly would have gotten some sort of kitchen implement or Dad's belt across the butt if she had, but there was nothing but silence about the topic from that moment on from her and my parents. The silence was almost worse than being punished; I kept waiting for the punishment that never came. But the topic never came up again until about forty years later when my aunt Sandra, Mrs. Mohl's daughter, and I were chatting on the phone one time.

Sandra and my mom had been good friends when they were in high school, and I had always been close to my aunt. After my mom died, our relationship tightened. I was so honoured and warmed when, after my mom passed away and I was talking on the phone with my aunt, she asked me, "Would it be okay if I kept phoning you now and then? You are a lot like your mom, and I will really miss your mom."

Would it? Absolutely! I have always deeply valued my relationships with my extended family members, and fond memories of the Easter treats Auntie Sandra always gave me and my sister when they came to visit from Calgary will stay with me for life.

Nut Bags and Num-Nums

In our phone chats after Mom died, my aunt and I often talked about her mom and mine, about getting older, about caring for aging parents, about death. Her mom had passed away several years before mine did, and her father was aging, as was mine. Even though we were a generation apart, we could relate to each other; we were taking care of one aging parent while mourning the loss of the other after watching them decline.

After she finished sharing a memory of her mom, I told her, "I have a funny story about your mom. I don't know if you've ever heard this but I love this story."

I relayed to her the Chicken Salad Sandwich story, and as I ended, she giggled.

"I've always wondered if your mom told my mom about that," I told her, "but I suspect she didn't because I'm sure I would have been spanked good and hard over that one. Or maybe she did tell her and the two of them just had a laugh about it, but yeah, I'll never know if my mom ever heard about that incident."

She was still giggling. "Mom never told me that story, but that's a good one."

Learning Useful Words

As I worked my way through elementary and junior high school, I started to speak up more in class, but I remained extremely self-conscious until late in junior high school. I rarely raised my hand in class to answer questions. One reason was because I didn't want to speak. But also, even now, I need a lot of thinking time before I know what I want to say. By the time I had formulated a response to a teacher's question, someone else had answered and the discussion had moved on. As I got older though, I wanted to be more outgoing so I started to try to participate in class more.

In Science class one day in grade four, for some reason, Miss Laverty was asking what happens when someone gets a nosebleed. I guess she was trying to teach us about blood clotting (why?). When she asked what happens if your nosebleed stops but you blow your nose, no one stuck up their hand. I raised mine.

I know the answer!

"Yes, Lorna. Do you know what comes out of your nose after a nosebleed?"

"A big, bloody booger."

My classmates all burst out laughing, and my face burned with embarrassment.

Nut Bags and Num-Nums

Why are they laughing? I am not wrong! I said to myself.

"Yes, that's a blood clot."

Ah. "*Clot*."

A new word.

In grade seven Language Arts class, our teacher had us read the short story, *The Dog of Pompeii* by Louis Untermeyer. Before we started the story, our teacher was trying to set the context so he asked, "Who knows where Pompeii is?"

No one put up their hand so I gave it a go.

"Yes, Lorna?"

"India," I replied.

Again, everyone laughed.

I wasn't as confident in my answer this time, but I got annoyed at my classmates and thought, *Why are you all laughing at me? You didn't know either. I didn't see anyone else try to answer!*

He kindly corrected me.

"No, Lorna, you're thinking of Bombay. Pompeii is in Italy," and he proceeded to tell us about the disastrous eruption of Mount Vesuvius.

My classmates' laugher stuck with me, but what I was most focused on was the story of the dog, Bimbo, and the eruption.

Nut Bags and Num-Nums

Wow! So, people were going about their daily business when they were suddenly killed in this disaster. Bodies of family members frozen in time as they were hugging each other. In Pompeii today, you can see petrified loaves of freshly baked bread, fossilized animals. It's like the story in the Bible of Lot's wife being instantly turned into a pillar of salt when she looked back as they were running away from Sodom. I think I'd like to see Pompeii!

I thought about the March 1980 eruption of Mount St. Helens in Washington, occurring less than a year prior. Washington State seemed so far away from Alberta yet, a few days after hearing about the eruption on the news, I noticed a fine, chalky, grey dust in the air. It settled on the ground, on my parents' vehicles, and on every other outdoor surface. I ran my finger through the fine layer of ash on Mom's car, fascinated that ash from a volcanic eruption so far away had settled in our farmyard. On the prairie, volcanos seemed so foreign—so distant, because we were a good five-hour-drive from the mountains—yet our lives felt the impact of this eruption, albeit minor. I was interested in geology by this time and wondered what it would be like to see a volcanic eruption.

And I remembered my dogs, Frisky and Charlie, who had been killed several years prior. I could relate to the story of a young boy and his dog—the tight bond they formed. In the climax of the story, Tito cried out for Bimbo and remained inconsolable that they had been separated forever, Bimbo making the ultimate sacrifice by going back to retrieve some baking for Tito and getting caught in the lava flow.

I know exactly how Tito felt, knowing he was never going to play with his dog again, I thought.

Nut Bags and Num-Nums

The imagery of this story, the emotion I felt as we studied it, and the mystery of Pompeii—a city frozen in time and available for the public to see—left a great impression on me. I made it a goal to see this great archaeological site one day.

***

Despite not knowing the word for blood clot when I was eight, I did know quite a few other words that I had learned from my dad.

Whenever I escaped the house and joined my dad outside, I wanted to help him with the cattle, horses, and other farm duties. I retrieved tools for him, opened gates, held vaccination guns, and so on. If there was nothing I could help with, I hovered and watched. And learned.

Many of my childhood memories include watching my dad castrate, de-horn, vaccinate, or brand a bovine; help a cow birth a calf; or move an animal from one barn stall to a corral or pasture. Of course, animals don't understand when you are trying to help them. My dad had a temper, and he often lost it when dealing with unruly livestock.

Even before I was five, I knew there were a lot of words that came out of my dad's mouth that I was never supposed to say: damn, dammit, goddamn it, sonofabitch, Jesus Christ ..., but one in particular confused me: cocksucker. I knew that cock was another word for rooster, but I had no idea why this word was so bad that I was never to utter it. Ever.

What is so bad about roosters? I wondered. *We have them on the farm and we talk about them all the time.*

Nut Bags and Num-Nums

When I was around ten, I learned that my dad was *not* referring to roosters.

For some reason, though, "shit" wasn't off limits, apparently.

My uncle told me this story when I was well into my forties. I have no recollection of the event because according to him, I was three when it happened.

"I remember it clear as day," he told me. "Your other uncle and I wanted to hunt prairie chicken on your dad's land. He and I and your aunts got into the car and drove around some of your dad's pastureland several miles away from the farmyard. You came with us. We were driving along the fence line looking for chickens and at one point, we decided to get out of the car and walk through the pasture to try to flush prairie chickens out of the underbrush. The five of us were walking through the brush when you decided to be helpful. You saw your prim and proper and very religious aunt getting close to a cow pie on the ground and warned her, 'Careful you don't step in that cow shit over there.' That was probably the most we ever heard you say in the first five years of your life."

My uncle still laughs his ass off whenever he tells me this story. My mom was surely mortified when we came back to the house and my uncle told her what I had said.

***

Mom always referred to my dad's profane outbursts as his "words". Whenever Mom came into the house after helping Dad with the cattle, Janice and I asked ask how things had gone.

Nut Bags and Num-Nums

"Well, there were a lot of words," was her usual reply.

I loved joining my parents on day trips to Stettler, roughly an hour's drive northwest of Hanna. Stettler was, and still is, a bit bigger than Hanna so it had more stores and restaurants. Going to the music store in Stettler was always on our list so that I could spend my allowance on a cassette tape, LP, or 45 and take some of my favourite music home to listen to.

We also stopped at the A&W every time we went to Stettler. Hanna didn't have one, and the frosty mugs of root beer were a big treat.

The A&W was a drive-up. Dad parked the car and ordered our food through the radio. I waited impatiently in the back seat for our root beer and burgers.

There was an unforeseen incident though when all four of us decided to get root beer floats instead of pop. When our order came, Dad started in on his float while Mom passed floats and burgers to me and my sister in the back seat.

"GODDAMSONOFABITCH!"

My dad let out a stream of his words from the front seat after dousing his lap with root beer.

Mom turned her head back to me and Janice and cheerfully warned us, "Don't push on your ice cream, girls!"

***

Nut Bags and Num-Nums

Besides the words that Dad used when he was frustrated with cattle, he also had just as many quips and funny sayings that became family jokes over the years.

My mom was prone to sinus infections and migraines. When we were kids, Janice and I knew that if Mom was still in bed when we got up in the morning, it was going to be a quiet day and we likely wouldn't see her until late afternoon or evening, if at all that day. We were to be quiet on the days she was in bed.

One of her sinus infections had her knocked out for three days, and on the fourth morning, she finally got out of bed and sat down at the dining room table to have some dry toast for breakfast. As she sat at her spot, head in her hands, staring down at her toast trying to muster up the desire to eat it, Dad tried to be thoughtful.

"You want some peanut butter with that?" he asked.

Mom's head shot up.

"Harvey! I've been so stuffed up I've barely been able to breathe for three days. Do you really think I want peanut butter sticking to my mouth and throat on top everything else?"

Poor Dad. He was only trying to help make her toast more appealing.

I was in university when this next incident happened, so I wasn't witness to it but this is the story as Mom told it to me:

"I was in bed with one of my migraines, so I didn't want your dad bugging me. Remember, he had never done any of the

Nut Bags and Num-Nums

cooking up to that point except for barbecuing steaks, but he wanted his damn baking powder biscuits, so I told him he had to make them himself. I got up and pulled the recipe out for him. And then I went back to bed. There was so much banging going on in the kitchen though, after a while I couldn't stand it any more so I finally got up to see what on earth he was doing. When I got to the kitchen, Dad was just taking the biscuits out of the oven. They looked exactly like hockey pucks," she told me. "Same shape, same size, same colour. They went into the garbage."

Day two. Mom was still in bed with the migraine.

CLANG CLANG BANG CLANG in the kitchen. Dad was trying again.

As Mom was telling me this story, the image that came to mind was that of the Swedish Chef from The Muppet Show but with my dad's face.

"The second batch was a little better, but they were still as dry as a fart," she told me. "But he ate them."

Mom remained in bed for a third day, and on the third day, Dad created biscuits.

"I was feeling a little better so I got up to see how this process was progressing."

Again, she got to the dining room just as Dad was taking his biscuits out of the oven.

"Lorna, on this third try, they were better than I have ever made them," she admitted to me.

Nut Bags and Num-Nums

From that point on, Dad was in charge of making the baking powder biscuits.

***

Even with the impact of severe dementia, Dad's temper prevailed. When I was at his senior's residence clearing out his room several days after he passed away, one by one, staff members came to give me their condolences and tell me how much they enjoyed my dad. They all commented on how much they would miss his loud laughter and bright blue eyes.

"But we also knew when he was angry," one of the staffers told me. "One of my colleagues was in charge of giving him his showers. Most times he was fine, but sometimes he got mad. He would sit in the shower on the chair and swear the whole time. So many bad words!"

I laughed.

"Yup. That's him!"

What Clutch?

My dad was mainly a rancher, but he did some farming, as well. He kept most of his crops as feed for the cattle and horses in the winter, but he also grew enough that he had some grain and bales to sell in the fall. And just as brandings were community events when all the neighbours pitched in to get the work done quickly and efficiently, neighbours and family also helped with getting the crops in so that the work would get done before the weather turned.

My mom's dad was a farmer who did a bit of ranching; he was the opposite of my dad because the soil where his farm was located was better suited for growing grain crops than running cattle on it as pastureland. He retired from the farm when I was five. Because of his vast experience, he was an expert to be relied on when harvest came. He and Grandma drove out to the farm, and Grandpa worked with my dad while Grandma helped Mom in the kitchen. Mom and Grandma also often drove the grain truck back and forth between farm and field so that Grandpa and Dad could keep going in the tractor combining, swathing, or baling. Mom and Grandma usually did double duty, taking meals to the two men when they drove back to the field with the grain truck to load it up with oats, wheat, or barley, which they then drove back to the farm. When they arrived with the grain truck, Janice and I helped unload the grain and get it into the granaries.

She and I both learned to drive the farm half-ton truck much earlier than what was legally allowed. Dad needed us to bring him some medicine for a sick animal, or Mom was busy in the house and couldn't take lunch out to the field during harvest. Of course we never drove on the highways until we were legally allowed to, but we learned to drive according to the 4-H motto: "Learn to Do by Doing." We jumped into the truck and figured out how to drive by trial and error.

But all the cars and half-ton or three-quarter ton trucks Mom and Dad owned over the years were automatic. The grain truck had a manual transmission. Because we had taught ourselves to drive simply by doing so, I guess Dad assumed the same would happen when he asked Janice to drive the grain truck over to the other side of the yard one day. She hopped in and tried to start the truck. After a few minutes of grinding and jolting and head-scratching, she hollered at Dad, "I can't get the truck to move!"

"For God's sakes, use the clutch!" Dad bellowed back.

"What clutch?"

Dad burst out laughing. This was one time he had to actually give her a driving lesson.

Sometimes I tagged along in the grain truck with my mom out to the field, especially when she was taking lunch or supper to my dad and grandpa. We enjoyed a brief family picnic in the field before everyone got back to work.

I've always been fascinated with space, and I love gazing at the full moon or a full sky of stars. On the wide-open prairie on a clear night, the sky can be mysterious and dazzling and seemingly endless with all that is twinkling and glowing.

I was in the passenger seat of the grain truck while Mom was driving from the field back to the farm. I hung my head out the window, neck craned as I took in the beauty of a clear, night sky. I was in awe.

"Look at all them stars!" I commented.

"Lots of them up there, eh?" Mom replied.

"Yup."

For years after that, whenever I was with my mom on a clear summer or fall evening, she would point out to me the night sky and say, "Look at all them stars up there."

These days, when I look up at the night sky, I imagine that my mom is one of those stars looking down on me ... I'm sure she's the one that's twinkling the brightest.

Wilbur

Every year, we had two or three pigs. After my sister and I had read *Charlotte's Web*, every year we named one of our pigs Wilbur. And every year, Wilbur or one of his pals got shot, scalded, gutted, cut in half, chopped up, wrapped up, and tossed into the freezer. We butchered one pig per year for ourselves and sold the others.

Wilbur and friends had their own stinky mud house toward the back of our farmyard. Among my sister's and my farm chores was to feed the pigs. Their slop was made up of chopped wheat chaff, milk or water, and any kitchen scraps that might be up for grabs—mostly vegetable peelings. But pigs eat pretty much everything. Sometimes we fed them a wee bit of coal because they loved it, and listening to them crunch it was fun.

And as they munched and grunted through their meals, we watched them eat. Often, we scratched them with a stick on the top of the head, behind the ears, or on the back or butt. If they wanted their butts scratched, they turned around and gave us a full view, wiggling their hams and curly tails. Throughout my childhood, I always thought that pigs were the happiest, most content animals on the planet. You need only feed them and give them a bit of love, and they thrived.

Butchering a pig and a yearling steer or heifer was a much bigger undertaking than butchering chickens. We were dealing

Nut Bags and Num-Nums

with one animal rather than a hundred, but the size of the larger animals also made it a more complicated process.

These skills are often passed down through the generations. But my dad was a city kid. He grew up in Medicine Hat and was a teenager when my grandparents moved up to the Hanna area and bought their farm.

Shortly after moving, he started working for other farmers and ranchers in the area as a hired hand and quickly built up his skills. One of the local farmers he worked for as a young man was my mom's dad, which is how he and my mom met.

Soon after we moved into the new house, my dad took a course on meat cutting. He hung a large chart on the wall of the old house—a picture of a bovine with lines through it indicating where all the different cuts were portioned out.

Dad did the heavy lifting—literally—by killing the larger animals, skinning them, and cutting the carcass in half. Once it was halved, he let it hang for the required amount of time for it to cure. When each half was ready to be cut into individual cuts, he mobilized his team: Mom, Janice, and me.

We always did the butchering in January for a few reasons. It was after Christmas, so life was a lot less hectic than it was in November and December. Winters were always slow for Dad as there were no crops to tend to, and in January, the cows had not yet started to give birth. And January was sure to be cold, ensuring that the meat was cold regardless of where it was kept.

Ah yes, the cold.

Nut Bags and Num-Nums

Helping with the butchering required being bundled in my parka, standing for hours in the old house, cutting cold meat with my bare hands and a razer-sharp knife. It wasn't possible to use gloves, so our hands were chilled to the bone while we spent hours cutting up meat. When I was younger, my main tasks were to cut up the chunks of meat thrown my way into cubes for stewing meat or into smaller chunks so that they could be run through the meat grinder to make hamburger. As I got older, I was entrusted with the finer cuts such as steaks and roasts. Dad cut them and then passed them my way so I could trim extra fat.

Cold as my hands were, I didn't complain. I knew there was no point. I had no choice. On a farm, there are times and tasks when "all hands are on deck," and butchering season was one of those times. Besides, I loved my steak and burgers, and even when I was young, I recognized and appreciated that my parents were working hard to put wholesome food on our table. A burger tastes all that much better when you know you helped your father create the meal.

***

We used scraps of meat to make hamburger but also sausage. My ancestry goes back to Germany on both sides for as far as anyone has been able to trace (about a thousand years on Mom's side). So, of course sausage was a mainstay of our diet. Sometimes we made sausage in the old house but often we did it in the basement of the new house. Sausage making does not require the same sub-Arctic temperatures that butchering and cutting meat does.

Nut Bags and Num-Nums

Often my grandparents came to help with the sausage making. Sometimes, if some of my aunts and uncles were visiting, they helped out, too.

The meat had to be kept cold until we made the sausage, but once we hauled it out of the fridge, my dad plopped it into a huge bowl or bin and mixed in the appropriate spices. Sadly, I never learned the secret recipe, but there really wasn't one. He added spices and mixed everything by hand until it tasted right. After mixing the meat and spices thoroughly, my dad or grandpa took a small handful of the mixture, flattened it out into a patty, and plopped it into a frying pan on the hot plate. We each got a small sample to see if the meat to spice ratio was right. If not, Dad or Grandpa made adjustments and then fried another sample. Repeat until they had it right.

When the mixture passed the taste test, it was time to make the actual sausages. Here's when I was put into action.

My parents used real intestines for sausage casings, but they didn't make the casings themselves. Can you imagine the work involved in pulling the intestines out of an animal and cleaning them satisfactorily so that they could be used for sausage casings? My parents were hard working and frugal, but they were also rational. They had their limits. They bought their casings from a butcher shop. For me, running my fingers through a bowl of slippery animal guts soaking in water was always fun and prompted a few squeals.

When I was little, I was only able to put the meat into the machine but when I got older, I operated the machine's hand crank. Dad expertly guided the meat as it came out the other end and into the casings, creating sausage snakes. He either cured them for several days in an old refrigerator that he had converted into a smoker or immediately packaged and froze them.

We made two kinds of sausage: regular garlic sausage and my favourite, leberwurst (liver sausage). I wasn't particularly fond of liver when I was a kid so I don't know why I was so crazy about the leberwurst. I was thrilled any time I woke up to the smell of Mom cooking it for breakfast.

My favourite, though, was my grandpa's sausage, which was cured and dried to become similar to a thick pepperoni stick. It wasn't quite as dry as the store-bought pepperoni sticks, and it had a smoky, meaty flavour that I've never tasted in anything else I've ever eaten. As a kid, I would happily bypass the cookies and gnaw on a piece of Grandpa's dried sausage as an after-school snack.

We attended the Evangelical church, but I had several Lutheran friends. Every year, even now, the German men in the Lutheran church make homemade sausage and serve it on Shrove Tuesday with the traditional pancakes. Of course it was purely psychological but to me, my family's sausage always tasted a smidge better than the Lutherans'. Regardless, I've never tasted sausage as good as what all these German men made.

Made with Love

When I was in my early forties and my mom was dying, I prepared for her funeral by practicing the song I chose to sing at her funeral: Dolly Parton's "Coat of Many Colors." I know Dolly wrote this song about her childhood, but even when I first heard it in my own childhood, I felt like she was singing about me. My mom sewed a lot clothes for my sister and me, and for the first ten years of my life, most of my clothes were hand-me-downs from Janice.

In addition to Mom's homemade shirts, pants, and dresses, home-knitted mittens and toques from my grandmas, and homemade quilts on our beds, our food was also homegrown. My mom went to town once a week or less for groceries, and most of what was on her grocery list were items we couldn't make or grow ourselves such as toilet paper and light bulbs.

Mom always grew a huge garden. When we lived in the old house, the garden plot was a fairly large chunk of space in front of the house. In my stylish blue, handmade Fortrel bell-bottom pants I crouched down and picked strawberries for my mom while Charlie and Frisky romped around beside me. For every berry that made it into the bowl, another found its way to my mouth.

When we moved to the new house, Dad built Mom a greenhouse and rototilled a large new section of garden. Mom alternated over the years using one of the large garden spots for potatoes only and the other for additional vegetables.

She and Dad taught my sister and me at an early age how to hill potatoes and to recognize the difference between the vegetables and weeds. Every summer, our main job was weeding, which of course we whined about. We did appreciate the results of the garden, though. Our family enjoyed the produce for several months, starting in June with lettuce salad. Our German heritage dictated that leaf lettuce was to be mixed with some chopped green onion and tossed with a dressing of cream, vinegar, salt, and pepper. To this day, whenever I get my hands on some leaf lettuce at a farmer's market, I buy some cream and make this salad.

Later in the summer when it came time to pick peas, a similar phenomenon happened as with the strawberries. For every few pods that landed in the pail, another somehow opened on the spot, and the green balls of goodness just happened to fall into my mouth. Sometimes when I was outside for other reasons, I found myself making a detour through the garden and helping myself a few pods off the pea plants. Mom always saw the evidence on the ground of both her daughters doing this, but we were never scolded. There were certainly worse things we could have been snacking on.

My favourite time and way to eat our garden potatoes was in early summer when baby potatoes are about the size of a golf ball. At that size and stage, they have such an earthy taste. Mom had her own recipe for these, too. She boiled them and then mixed them with a thick cream sauce and fresh parsley, also from the garden. "Parsley potatoes" is another summer delicacy

Nut Bags and Num-Nums

for me all these years later when I nab a bag of baby potatoes and some fresh parsley at a farmer's market.

From the time I started kindergarten all the way through high school, Mom allowed me and Janice to have an after-school snack. The most common snacks were cookies, which of course I loved, but one of my favourites was on the days when Mom baked bread. I especially loved fresh-from-the-oven, soft, warm, homemade bread slathered with butter and jam. My favourite combination was and still is butter with apricot jam. Raspberry, peach, and saskatoon jam are tied as my second favourites. Buying jam was unheard of. Instead, Mom bought fruit from the trucks that came through in the summer, and of course we picked raspberries and strawberries from our garden.

We had to go hunting for saskatoons. Our property didn't have saskatoon bushes on it, but my family had the right connections. Every summer, we went traipsing through the Hand Hills, a hilly area about thirty minutes southwest of Hanna, with Grandpa and Grandma Stuber and the right tools for the job: a plastic, one-gallon ice cream bucket attached to our waists with a belt or rope so that both hands were free for picking berries and steadying ourselves on the trees and bushes as we clomped through the coulees. My grandma was tiny—not even five feet tall—and inevitably, we lost sight of her in the bushes at some point during each outing. Mom and Dad were never worried about losing her entirely. She knew her way around a saskatoon patch and would eventually rustle her way out of the thick brush with a full bucket of purple berries.

The most important task, besides picking the berries, was to make sure I didn't tip my bucket and dump my haul onto the ground. As the bucket increased in weight, even a slight bump against a tree could cause the bucket to overturn.

Mom taught me the art of berry-picking.

"Wrap your fingers around the stem just above the berries like this," she showed me. "Then, pull a little, but not so much that you squash the berries. They will let go of the stem and fall into the bucket."

She pointed out to me which ones were ideal for picking.

"The ones that are starting to shrivel up aren't worth picking. Look for ones that are round, large, and such a dark purple that they looked almost black. If they are still a little bit green, leave them. They aren't ready yet."

The soft thud of the berries hitting the bottom of the ice cream bucket signalled that I was on my way to getting a gallon of delicious treats to take home and eat with cream or ice cream or help my mom turn into jam, sauce, pie, or kuchen.

When we returned home, the trunk of the car contained several ice cream buckets filled to the brim. The fun part was over, and the tedious work then had to be done: sorting and cleaning the haul. Inevitably, the buckets had not only berries but also stems, leaves, bugs—dead and alive. And not all the berries in the buckets were the good ones, so Mom set me and Janice to work sitting at the kitchen counter or table. We put a couple handfuls onto a plate, and the sorting began. One by one, we placed the good berries into another bucket and sent the leaves, stems, and shrivelled-up berries into a bowl, which Mom eventually dumped into the garden as compost. I hated this part because it took so long and was hideously boring compared to being outside exploring the saskatoon patch, but I knew it was a necessary part of getting us to the point of being able to enjoy the fruit.

And as soon as we had enough good berries, we got a treat of saskatoon berries in a bowl with cold, farm cream or homemade ice cream.

***

In my early elementary school years, we had two milk cows named Jersey and Lucy. Jersey was … a jersey cow. The calm, tawny-coloured cow with black hair around her eyes. For some reason, the Hereford milk cow got a human name: Lucy.

When I was old enough, one of my chores was milking Lucy in the morning and evening. No deviating from the schedule. If I was a few minutes late in getting out of the house with the pail, my mother's tongue would remind me of my duties.

"It's seven o'clock, Lorna. Time to milk the cow. You have to milk her on schedule. You also have homework to do. Get going with the milking so you can get the milk separated and feed the pigs and still have time to do your homework before it gets too late."

Last-Minute Lorna often needed a kick in the bum to put down whichever book she was reading and get the chores done.

We always had much more milk than we drank or used ourselves. The extra went to the chickens, pigs, cats, and dogs.

We also usually had more cream than we could use, and Mom sold it to people in town, who were thrilled to get a pint or quart of fresh, unpasteurized farm cream. Mom had a steady list of clientele who had regular orders for both cream and eggs.

Mom made homemade cottage cheese from the milk. Making cottage cheese was easy. She put a bowl full of milk on the counter and let it sit for several days until it curdled and the curds separated from a milky-looking water. Once it was the right consistency, she strained it through a kitchen towel, catching the curds. She twisted the kitchen towel so that the ball of curds was in the bottom of the towel and it created an upside-down ghost-like shape. She squeezed and twisted the towel to get as much liquid out as possible. She then put the cheese in a container and kept it in the fridge until we used it.

There were a few ways we loved to eat the cottage cheese. The first and easiest was mixed with a bit of cream along with some chopped green onion and salt and pepper. Lots of pepper for me!

This same concoction was what Mom and my grandmas used for filling for kase knefla—cottage cheese perogies. These, too, were a favourite family recipe. Mom made the filling and dough, formed the perogies, pinched them shut, and then cooked them in a pot of boiling water. When the perogies were cooked through, she pulled them out of the boiling water and either froze them or, if they were for our meal that day, transferred them to a frying pan, where she fried them in melted butter with bread crumbs. Once both the perogies and chunks of bread were nice and brown on each side, they were ready.

Nut Bags and Num-Nums

Until I was an adult, I had never heard of eating perogies that were only boiled, not fried, and I didn't know they could be filled with anything other than cottage cheese. When I went to Poland in my early forties, I ate my way through the options of perogies by sampling a different kind every day: blueberry, chocolate, meat, cottage cheese, cheddar cheese, potato, and more.

The pièce de résistance, though, when it came to using our milk and cream was the homemade ice cream. We almost always had ice cream in the freezer because it was a great way to use up extra milk and eggs, and because who doesn't love ice cream?

Mom usually made vanilla or chocolate. Although the chocolate was my favourite, I also enjoyed vanilla when we could mix fruit with it.

Sometimes Mom used the ice cream to make milkshakes.

Dad always used to comment, "Sure is peaceful out here," when talking about our farm. The closest farm was the neighbours who were two miles away cross country; we could see their farm from our house but we had to drive ten or fifteen minutes on the highway to get to their farm. And no one ever came down our road except to visit us or if they were lost. Ours was the only farm on the road.

When we made milkshakes, Mom always enjoyed hers to the last drop, slurping and sucking on the straw, making a heck of a noise trying to get every bit out of the bottom of the glass.

"Sure is peaceful out here!" she joked, using one of Dad's catch-phrases. She smirked as she slurped and sucked.

"Yeah, it is, until YOU decide to have a milkshake!" my dad snorted to her.

***

When I was in my teens, Lucy was getting old and so we sold her. Jersey had gone down the road a few years earlier. Being without a milk cow was, to me, completely unacceptable. I had come to take for granted the homemade cottage cheese, butter, and ice cream, not to mention the milk we put on our cereal and the cream we used for the lettuce salad and to pour over a bowl of peach slices or saskatoons in the summer. We needed a new milk cow. My parents resisted getting one, but I kept forcing the issue. I had some money saved up, and I was old enough to start managing it.

"Why don't I buy a milk cow? I have enough money to pay for one, and then the cow is my responsibility. I will do the milking and we can still have the milk and cream."

"You aren't buying a milk cow. We are fine without one."

"No, we're not! Mom, you are buying ice cream, milk, and cream. Why? We can make our own. And the store-bought stuff doesn't taste nearly as good. I want to buy a milk cow."

My parents finally gave in to my relentless nagging, and we went in search of a new milk cow. We bought one from some neighbours, and I resumed my twice-a-day chore of milking and separating the milk from the cream. The new element in all of this was, because the cow was mine, I was able to pocket the money for the cream sales.

Nut Bags and Num-Nums

I was in the local 4-H club and our focus was horses, but we could also choose from some optional side projects. One that I chose was photography because I loved to take pictures. Shortly after getting into the photography option and learning a bit about the art, I realized my Kodak Instamatic wasn't going to cut it. I decided I wanted a nice camera, so I went shopping.

Berkes Jewellers in Hanna was also the camera shop. I looked at their offerings and settled on a nice Canon SLR. It cost around $200, which was more money than I had in my wallet or even bank account, so I negotiated a deal with the shop owner to pay off the camera over several months. My payments were to be in installments of $20 each.

My mom continued to sell the cream to townspeople and she gave me the money, which I then saved up and took to the store once a month to pay off my camera. Watching the shop worker pull out the index card with my tally on it, update it every time I made a payment, and then put it back into the drawer each month until ... finally, the balance reached zero gave me great satisfaction. The camera was fully mine!

Eat!

I was a lucky kid: I grew up ten minutes from both sets of grandparents as well as Emil and Rosie, my surrogate grandparents. Although all six of them had been born in Canada, my grandmas, and then my mom, carried on the tradition of having great German baking and meals. There was never a lack of food. My mom's mom was always nagging me to eat when I was a kid. I was a beanpole and she clearly thought I needed fattening up.

She insisted I go to the fridge and help myself to whatever I wanted whenever we visited, but my mom had taught me not to be so presumptuous as to go into someone else's fridge. Grandma always saw I was hesitant to open her fridge, so the moment we walked into her house, she brought out the cookies, cinnamon buns, squares, or any other treats that she had.

"Eat!" she always ordered me.

And so I did. She often had different treats than what my mom made. One thing was guaranteed; we could never leave her house empty-handed. She made sure we had cookies, bread, or cake to take home, or it might be a new toy or mittens she had knitted for us. Sometimes we left with socks, candy she'd found on sale, and later when I had left home, toilet paper. When toilet paper went on sale, she bought enough to give a package to each of her kids and grandkids. As a broke university student, I was grateful for these gifts.

Nut Bags and Num-Nums

Grandma Stuber's house was the same in that there was always baking around. She wasn't as forceful with almost shoving food down my throat, but she always had baking. She made the typical cookies like chocolate chip and oatmeal, but my favourites were those made from her German recipes. Two of Grandma Stuber's best treats were what we called keegla and plachinda. My parents had both learned German as their first language, and in fact, Mom told me that neither of them could speak English when they started school, and so remnants of the German culture, including language, were part of my and my grandparents' households when I was growing up. Since it was my great-grandparents who had immigrated to Canada, by the time I was born, the German language my parents and grandparents spoke had morphed; I knew their pronunciation wasn't authentic, and many of the words and phrases we used were derivatives of the real German expressions.

Keegla was a twisted donut made with a slightly sweet, unleavened dough. They were deep fried and we ate them plain. For me, the flavour of the dough was enough. I loved these knots of dough. When I went to Iceland in the spring of 2022, I was delightfully surprised to see items that looked exactly like my Grandma Stuber's keegla for sale in the coffee shops and bakeries. I tried one, and instantly the taste of my childhood filled my mouth again.

Why are these treats in Iceland? We are German!

I asked a tour guide and he explained that they were a local favourite but they had originated in Germany. I was astonished that the only two places in the world I had ever seen these donuts were in my Grandma Stuber's house and in practically every bakery I entered in Iceland.

Plachinda was made with a similar dough but it was used to form a turnover with a spiced pumpkin filling. Not sweet like pumpkin pie, but savoury. The pumpkin puree was mixed with sauteed onion, pepper, and other spices. I searched online several years ago and managed to find a recipe for these. I made them and they were good, but nothing is a match for a grandmother's baking.

A couple of other favourites that my mom and both grandmas made were strudels and kuchen. We never had the sweet kind of strudels—the dessert pastries found in bakeries; if Mom made something like that, they were just turnovers. Our strudels were made from dough that is stretched so thin until we could see through it, then rolled up until the roll is one inch thick. Mom and Grandma then cut them in three-inch strips. Mom steamed them on top of chicken or beef stew, and it was required that the strudels be topped with Roger's Golden Syrup. To eat them without the syrup was just not acceptable, nor was eating them with any other syrup.

Once I had settled in Calgary in my mid-twenties, my parents and some other family members started a tradition of getting together in another small Alberta town for dinner. Carbon, Alberta, is about fifty miles east of Calgary, roughly half way to Hanna. For several years, one of the restaurants in Carbon was owned by a couple who had regular food on the menu, but once a year, they had "German Days" for a weekend buffet that included schnitzel, sausage, red cabbage, and strudels. Every year that my family made a reservation, I drove out from Calgary to meet them and enjoy a good meal. The first year we went, I noticed a crucial ingredient was missing. I made a mental note and gave myself some homework. Starting the second year, and every year thereafter, I brought along a bottle of Roger's Golden Syrup for our family to use for our strudels. The restaurant owners didn't mind in the least.

Roger's Golden Syrup was a staple in our house during my childhood. If there were no cookies or jam bread available for after-school snacks, another option was to scoop a large spoonful of peanut butter into a bowl, and add an equal amount of Roger's Golden Syrup. Stir it up to mix it together and voila, snack. I ate this on many an occasion and I've often thought that eating this after school as much as I did was the reason I never was a fan of peanut butter when I moved away from home. I'm sure the richness of this snack turned me off of peanut butter for a couple of decades in my early adult years.

Kuchen is the German word for cake, and here too, by the time I came along, my family had morphed the language. "Kooka" was a constant in our house. In Germany, cake of any kind is acceptable for coffee and cake time, 4:00pm each day. In our house, kooka was a certain type of cake. The crust was a yeast dough pressed into pie pans. On top we placed fruit: plums, peaches, cherries, saskatoons, or apples. Then, we drizzled a cream and egg mixture over the fruit and topped that with a crumble of flour, sugar, cinnamon, and butter. One of my family favourites was kase (cheese) kuchen—cottage cheese kooka. Instead of fruit, Mom or Grandma sprinkled a mixture of dried cottage cheese and cream on the dough, with the crumble topping of sugar, cinnamon, flour, and butter. Of course they used homemade cottage cheese. My dad loved plum kuchen; my other favourites were peach or saskatoon. Making kooka was an all-day affair, and the recipe turned out around ten or twelve of the delicious cakes. That meant we got one for dessert at supper that night and several went into the freezer.

We rarely ate out. Why drive to town to eat in a restaurant when the freezer is full of homegrown beef, pork, chicken, turkey, and vegetables and in the summer, the vegetables are all fresh for the taking from the garden?

One rare exception was on Mother's Day. Every Mother's Day, we piled into the car and Dad drove us to Castor to have dinner at The Shangri-La. I don't know why this tradition began as, there was a Chinese restaurant in Hanna: The York. But for some reason, probably just to make it an extra treat for Mom, we went forty-five minutes farther up the highway. Not only was it wonderful to go so far away, but we got to eat out, and we got Chinese food, which we all loved. There was an extra treat in the mix for me and my sister: We were allowed to order Shirley Temples on this special occasion.

I was skinny when I was a kid, and in fact, one of my mom's nicknames for me was Skinny Minnie. It wasn't long after sitting down for a meal that I would start to pick at my food, not because I was a fussy eater, but because I seemed to get full quickly. Many a time I was force feeding myself, trying to clean my plate as instructed.

"You can't leave the table until your plate is empty," was my mom's rule, and it was gruelling. I tried so hard, but there were times I would put the last bite or two of food in my mouth and just hold it inside my cheek like a chipmunk.

"What are you doing? Swallow your food," my mom instructed me.

"There's nowhere for it to go," I replied as I sat there, cheeks bulging.

This quickly became a running joke, and when Mom saw me sitting there, meal after meal, cheeks bulging, she teased me. As an adult, if I left a bit of food on my plate, she always made the same comment.

"Nowhere for it go to?" she asked.

"No," I whined.

But Janice and I were never allowed to leave the table until plate and cheeks were empty.

I wasn't—and still am not—a picky eater, but I knew kids were supposed to hate things like broccoli and liver. In solidarity with my older sister, I refused to eat my liver whenever it was on the menu. No matter. The same rules applied. We had to sit at the table until our plates were empty. I knew that the liver was less appealing when it was cold and that we should just buckle down and eat it when it was still hot, but I was stubborn, and so I followed Janice's lead and sat there as long as we could stand it.

One night when we were having liver for supper, she and I made a big scene out of having to stay at the table until our liver was in our bellies. We added ketchup (that only made it worse), we cut it into tiny pieces and tried to eat it one mini bite at a time. We were being dramatic and silly more than anything, and

Nut Bags and Num-Nums

Mom was getting tired of our antics. She left the kitchen and went to the basement. A minute later she came back.

As soon as she re-entered the kitchen, the phone rang. Since we were banished to the table, Mom answered the phone.

"Hello? Oh hi Maryanne. No, Janice can't come to the phone right now but I will tell her you called."

Click.

Maryanne was Janice's best friend, and when they were teenagers, talking on the phone was a huge and important part of their lives. Janice quickly downed her liver and got up to phone Maryanne back. Except ....

At that time, our phone was a party line and was connected to a live phone line in an abandoned farm alongside the highway. My sister had figured out that this phone was still working, and so there were times she would get on her horse, ride the three miles one way down to the abandoned farm and phone Maryanne from there so they could talk in private. It was hard for a teenager to have a private phone conversation in our house. Even though we had two phones, voices could be heard throughout the house, so it was guaranteed that someone would hear Janice's side of the conversation. Plus, if Mom knew Janice was on the phone, she often snuck to the other phone to listen in on the conversation. If Janice rode down to the other farmstead, Mom wouldn't know she was on the phone and wouldn't be tempted to pick up the other phone and listen in.

The other trick we knew was how to phone ourselves. Mom knew that if she picked up the receiver, dialed 123, waited a moment, and then put the receiver back on the hook, the phone would ring but no one would be on the other end.

In the midst of our liver standoff that night, she had snuck downstairs, dialed 123, and gotten back upstairs by the time our phone rang. When it rang, no one was calling; in an attempt to prompt Janice to down her liver, Mom had pretended Maryanne was phoning. It worked, but only once.

Bugg-y Crocuses and Num-Nums

My mom took pride in keeping the farm tidy and pretty. She made sure the fences and buildings were painted. Once I was old enough to tackle it, painting became one of my summer jobs. Mom was adamant that I properly sand the old paint off before refreshing the look of the fences. It was a ton of work because there was a lot of wooden fence, but I liked my job; it was relaxing, easy, and quiet. I could spend hours outside doing the work, lost in my own mind with my dog beside me, not having to talk to another human.

Mom also grew lots of flowers and kept the trees in the yard trimmed and healthy. Another summer job she delegated to Janice and me was weeding. We whined about weeding because we were kids and that's what kids do, but truth be told, I didn't mind the weeding for the same reasons I enjoyed painting the fence. It got me outside digging around in the dirt and enjoying a relaxing, quiet activity. It also helped knowing I was helping my mom beautify the yard and making space for the trees and vegetables to flourish by eliminating their competition.

Snapdragons grow easily on the prairie, and they come in a multitude of colours, so they were a great choice to beatify our farmyard. I was maybe four when Mom educated me on the secret of snapdragons when we were out in the garden one day.

"Come here. I want to show you something," she said.

Nut Bags and Num-Nums

I was poking around in the dirt with a stick, doing nothing useful. I went to stand beside her.

She bent over the snapdragon patch.

"Look."

She grasped the bottom of the flower of one of the snapdragons between her thumb and forefinger and squeezed.

"These are Num-Nums. When you push on the flower right here, it opens up. Num num num," she said in rhythm with the opening of the flower.

"It's like a mouth!" I said.

"Yes, so when you squeeze it like this, it's like the flower is saying 'num num'."

Snapdragons are, in my mind, forever known as Num-Nums.

One of my favourite flowers is the wild prairie crocus that grows in Alberta pastures in the spring. The fuzzy little purple flowers poke their heads out of the ground earlier than any other flower on the prairies. The sight of crocuses always indicates that winter is over.

At some point in my childhood, I started the tradition of picking the first crocuses I saw each year and bringing them back to my mom. I guess every child likes to give flowers to their mom. I went out on foot into the prairie to pick them as soon as spring arrived and I knew they would be blooming. If I was in the truck with my dad and we saw crocuses for the first time that spring, I got him to stop so I could jump out and pick some to take back for my mom. Later, when I got older and was able to go riding on my own, I set out on a day when I was sure I would see crocuses, riding my horse out onto the prairie for the sole purpose of making sure Mom got her springtime handful of prairie flowers.

Every year, she placed them in a cup of water on the dining room table, whether I brought her two or twenty. And as I got older, she teased me about bringing her more bugs than flowers. Yep, often the crocuses had itty-bitty critters in them, so in addition to admiring the crocuses, we also had to squish bugs when we were sitting at the table.

I continued this tradition every year until well into my thirties. As a young adult living in the city, more than two hours away from home, I didn't always get a chance to give Mom her springtime crocuses every year, but I made a point of picking them and giving them to her in the years that I could.

When I was at a Christmas market a few years ago, a local photographer had some framed prairie landscape photos for sale. A close-up of a bunch of crocuses in the field caught my eye. It was framed in barnboard, and the grey of the frame provided a nice contrast to the purple of those flowers. My mom had passed away a few years prior. I bought the picture and hung it on my wall as a reminder of my mom every time I look at it.

Oodles of Noodles

Mom and Dad didn't mill their own flour, so flour was one of the items on the grocery list when Mom went to town for supplies. But everything she made with flour was homemade: cakes, cookies, other desserts, cheese or cream sauces for our vegetables or noodles, and the noodles themselves. Twice a year, my mom put my sister, my dad, and me to work stocking up the pantry with homemade noodles.

Making pasta is easy: eggs, flour, and a bit of salt. Mix, roll, and put through the pasta machine to cut it.

Our homemade noodles served a dual purpose. They fed us, of course, but they were also a great way to use up extra eggs. Sometimes Mom planned a noodle-making day if we were running low on noodles, and sometimes she scheduled noodle-making to use up eggs. She usually gave some to each of my sets of grandparents whether they helped us or not.

My job until I was in my teens was "noodle runner." Mom mixed the dough, and she and Dad put it through the pasta machine. Janice and I were tasked with catching the fettuccini-sized noodles as they came out of the pasta machine and taking them to the living room, where Mom had set up a clothes rack and dining room chairs, both with towels on them. She also had lain bed sheets on the ground.

Nut Bags and Num-Nums

"Only take one handful at a time," Mom instructed us. "When you put the noodles on the towels or on the sheet, put each noodle down one at a time and make sure they don't touch each other. If they are touching, they will stick together and stay stuck together when they are dried."

On noodle-making day, it was impossible to use the living room as it was filled with chairs and the drying rack, and the floor was covered in noodles drying on the bedsheets. It took twenty-four hours for the noodles to dry. Once they were dry, Mom placed them in storage bins and buckets, securing the lids. She usually kept the noodles in a medium sized plastic garbage bin with a lid on it, and she also used one-gallon plastic ice cream buckets. She placed paper towel at the bottom of each storage container to absorb any remaining moisture and prevent mold.

Other than Kraft Dinner or the noodles in Campbell's soups, I didn't have commercially-made noodles until I was well into adulthood. Mom even sent me off to university with a couple ice cream buckets of homemade noodles. I love my KD, but there is nothing like the taste of homemade noodles. A bowl of homemade noodles with a bit of butter and salt is all I need for a meal.

One of my favourite ways to eat Mom's noodles was in her homemade chicken or turkey noodle soup. Because we had so much fresh and frozen farm-grown chicken and turkey, we had a steady supply of poultry carcasses to boil down for soup stock. Mom then made chicken or turkey noodle soup with chunks of meat that had been released from the bones, the stock, homemade noodles, and vegetables from the garden, including carrots, celery, onion, and potato. When I was in university, I used some store-bought egg noodles once to make homemade chicken noodle soup. But only once. There was no comparison in taste. After that, I started making my own noodles.

We never ate the homemade noodles fresh, for some reason. The purpose for spending an afternoon making them and then walking carefully around them for the next day in the living room was to stock up on dried noodles to use for the next several months. We did make a fresh type of pasta though, which we called "nefflies."

Neffla, nefflies, or gniftale, as I've seen it called in some old cookbooks, is basically our version of gnocchi. The closest real German word for it I have found is Schupfnudel:

> Schupfnudel (German; plural Schupfnudeln), also called Fingernudel (finger noodle), is a type of dumpling or thick noodle in southern German and Austrian cuisine. It is similar to the Central European kopytka and Italian gnocchi. They take various forms and can be referred to with a variety of names in different regions. They are usually made from rye or wheat flour and egg. Since the introduction of the potato to Germany in the seventeenth century, Schupfnudeln have also been made with potatoes. They are traditionally given their distinctive ovoid shape through hand-shaping. They are often served as a savoury dish with sauerkraut but are also served in sweet dishes.[3]

We made nefflies from the same ingredients as the dried noodles: egg, flour, salt. No potato was in the mix. The process

---

[3] "Wikipedia: Schupfnudel." Wikimedia Foundation. Last edited April 23, 2023. 16:56. en.wikipedia.org/wiki/Schupfnudel.

of mixing the dough was the same, but when it came time to roll out the dough, the goal was not to get it as thin as possible as it was for the strudels. Mom and my grandmas instead aimed for a thickness of about half an inch. Once the dough was rolled out, they cut it into strips of about half an inch wide. Then, they held each strip over a pot of boiling water while snipping pieces of the dough off, about one inch long or less, dropping the "dough boys", as we also called them, into the boiling water. The pieces of dough weren't the oblong shape of a finger that show up in pictures found in a Google search for Schupfnudel; they were the size and shape of gnocchi.

Once they were cooked through, Mom or my grandmas fried the nefflies in butter just as they did with the perogies so that they were crispy on the outside. Nefflies were a side dish and Mom almost always served them mixed in with sauerkraut, which we also made. Since we grew truckloads of potatoes, Mom or my grandmas fried chunks of potato with the dough and included cubed bread crumbs as well, as they did with perogies.

Until I was an adult, I had never heard the word gnocchi. We called these little bites of dough "rubber notchies" in addition to nefflies. I had always thought the term rubber notchies was a slam against them because they were more dense than regular noodles and could sometimes got a bit chewy. In retrospect, though, I suspect that the term notchies may be a bastardization of gnocchi.

In my late forties, I spent three weeks in Italy and of course thoroughly enjoyed a great many pasta meal. While I was in Florence, knowing the food and wine fame of Tuscany (all of Italy, really, but Tuscany drew my attention because of it's

Nut Bags and Num-Nums

reputation for good food and wine), I signed up for a one-day cooking course. Of course pasta was on the menu.

Hey, I know how to do this! I thought with a sense of satisfaction.

There were a few differences in how our instructor made pasta versus how my parents had taught me to make it. In our cooking course, we each got one egg—my parents used to use a dozen eggs or more. We made our own single-serving of pasta, which was fun, but in the end, everyone's pasta got dumped into the same pot of boiling water so we weren't necessarily eating our own pasta. But the point was to show us how to make the pasta with one egg and enough flour to form a firm, sticky dough.

Another difference was that once our ball of dough was formed, we were to let it rest for about half an hour. My parents never did this, and I'm not sure why.

And in Tuscany, we boiled our pasta fresh whereas my parents always dried our noodles. Still, the taste was almost the same (the only difference was probably because of whatever the Italian chicken ate versus what ours ate, thus determining the flavour of the egg)—delicious and satisfying.

The final difference was that, being in Italy, our pasta was topped with a homemade Bolognese sauce rather than butter and salt or cheese.

Growing up eating mostly homegrown or homemade food spoiled me for later in life. I still appreciate the taste of vegetables and meat from farmers or farmer's markets versus store-bought vegetables. The veggies I have grown in my own garden and that I still seek out at farmer's markets bring back fond memories of how hard my parents, my sister, and I worked to put healthy, wholesome, tasty food on the table.

Just Let Me Cut the Damn Apple

In 1982, along with a new body, a new 80s hairstyle, and new neon fashion, junior high school brought a batch of new teachers to my life and new school subjects.

I had a love-hate relationship with my Home Economics class and teacher. I loved cooking and sewing. Our teacher taught us exactly what she was supposed to, but I became a bit of a rebel in her class. For years, my mom had been teaching Janice and me to cook and sew, so I came to Home Ec. class with habits and knowledge I had picked up from my mom. Some of those details were wrong, according to my teacher.

The day we made apple pie, my teacher reprimanded me for cutting the apples into ¾ inch chunks instead of nice, long, slim slices. I had actually never had pie with sliced apples, only chunky ones. I recognized that she did make a good point in that the slimmer slices would take less time to bake, but I liked and was used to chunky apples in my pie.

Besides, who cares if it takes an additional ten minutes to bake? Does that really matter?

To her it did.

My Language Arts teacher was a new university graduate from Ontario and seemed somewhat out of place in this teeny town in rural Alberta, but he rolled with it all. I enjoyed his class because Language Arts and literature were and still are my passion, and he chose great stories and books for us. It was in his class that I decided to pick up where I had left off with the dog poem I had written for Miss Laverty and pursue my goal of becoming a writer.

One of our assignments in grade seven Language Arts class was to write an autobiography, and I took this assignment literally. While my classmates handed in one- or two-page summaries of their lives, I submitted a stack of paper, handwritten on loose leaf, twenty-eight pages long, depicting my life from birth to the moment I handed it in. I'm sure he was ecstatic to read pages and pages of my handwritten drivel; I got an A on it, probably simply because of its length.

I was at odds with him for two main issues, though. In junior high, as teenagers do, we were all experimenting with different aspects of our personalities, trying to figure out who we were. For one of my assignments, also handwritten (this was before computers existed, and I didn't yet know how to type), I wrote completely in capital letters. I got it back with a large red statement at the top, "Please do not write all in capital letters. Use proper capitalization and lower case." He also made this announcement to the class as he was handing back the assignments. I never knew if that announcement was directed only at me or if some of my classmates had done the same as I had done; writing in all caps was a bit of a trend at the time so I thought it was possible I wasn't the only one who had done this. Nevertheless, I followed orders from that point on, even though I was miffed.

Nut Bags and Num-Nums

He's stifling my creativity, I thought as I resigned myself to using proper lettering.

There was one incident that I never forgave him for: Lines.

Writing lines was a common punishment for minor offenses. It was easy for teachers to administer as it didn't require anything of them other than collecting a bunch of pages on which meaningless writing was scribbled a hundred times or more, the offender vowing to never commit the same offense again: I will/will not _____.

Language Arts was my favourite class, but it was my first class of the day. I'm not a morning person. Never have been, never will be. Even as a kid, I struggled to get out of bed early. When I was sent to bed at 7:00pm when I was five, I would lay in bed letting my imagination run wild for hours, taking me across the prairie and across the world. I eventually fell asleep, but not until I had been tossing and turning for hours. Over the decades, I have tried to reset my circadian rhythm. It just won't happen. My brain and body work best if I stay up late and get up late.

I'm sure I had been committing this sin for a while; I just wasn't aware of it. But one day, I was emitting my fourth yawn for that particular class period, and my teacher got fed up with me yawning in his class. I guess he took it personally and thought that meant his class was boring. And so he gave me lines.

I will not yawn in Language Arts.

I had to write this out two hundred times.

1. I will not yawn in Language Arts.
2. I will not yawn in Language Arts.

God forbid that you accidentally skip a line or two. If you got caught shortcutting, you had to do the assignment all over again but with more lines added to the task.

I was furious.

What is the point of doing this? It's a waste of time. A waste of ink. A waste of paper, I thought.

What made the task even more annoying was that as a leftie writing so many pages of redundant information, I ended up with the ball of my hand being stained in dark blue from the ink from my pen.

What I really wanted to write was a short personal essay:

I'm not yawning in your class because your class is boring. It's not boring. Language Arts is my favourite class. But I am a farm kid who gets up at six every morning to milk the cow, run the milk through the separator, and feed the pigs before I even have breakfast. Then, I get ready for school and ride the bus to get to school—a thirty-minute bus ride over ten miles; it takes ten minutes to get to town from our farm, but because of stops to pick up other kids and stopping at the elementary school first to drop off kids, I have to be ready to get on the bus by 8:00am. So the reason I'm yawning is because I'm tired after all of that. And you're punishing me for that?

But I bit my tongue, did my penance, and handed in his lines. And I made sure I didn't write them all in capital letters. I figured he'd make me redo them and add another two hundred if I pulled that stunt.

Nut Bags and Num-Nums

Mr. Ghidina was my Science teacher in junior high and while we had many good teachers in junior high, he was good *and* he was fun. I also had him for Chess, one of the options I took. From him, I learned essential life skills such as how to dissect an earthworm while keeping its multiple hearts intact and how to win a chess game in three moves. I also learned that it is possible to be goofy with your students while still maintaining a proper teacher-student relationship with them and being a damn good teacher.

Mr. Ghidina's wife was a substitute teacher for our school system, and so from time to time, we had lessons with her. It was during my junior high school years that their first child was born, and when we heard that the baby had come, some of my friends and I popped into the hospital to give our wishes to mother and baby.

The Guitar Man

Mom and Dad made sure we got involved in hobbies. And not just the self-directed hobbies my sister and I embraced, like collecting rocks.

"Let's go exploring," Janice often suggested.

Whether on horseback or on our own two legs, we loved exploring Dad's pastures. The land was full of rabbits, coyotes, badgers, and gophers running about. Other than the gophers we trapped, we didn't get too close to any of the critters, but we enjoyed watching them.

But there were also those pretty prairie crocuses and other flowers to discover. And rocks. Lots of rocks.

We had to help Dad pick rocks from the fields in the spring so that they wouldn't damage the equipment when he was seeding, haying, and combining, but we also picked up rocks from the cattle pastures and brought them back to the farmyard.

Janice introduced a new hobby to me. Perhaps she was trying to kill me; perhaps she was trying to introduce me to the wonders of geology. Who knows?

"Let's go to the garage and put the rocks in the vise grip. If we keep turning and turning, eventually the rocks will bust open, and then we can see what they look like inside."

"Okay," said the obedient one.

Seeing what the inside of those grey rocks looked like sounded cool.

And so we placed the rocks into the vise grip and cranked the handle, turning and turning until the rocks exploded. (Goggles? What are those?)

Once we saw that the insides of those rocks did look really cool, we collected more and more, looking for different types of rocks to see what they all contained within.

Mom supported our rock collecting hobby by buying us each a rock polishing kit as a Christmas gift, which we then used to smooth down and polish small rocks ... for what purpose? None except it was fun, and the smoothed rocks were neato.

(Note that nowhere have I mentioned that either of our parents told us that maybe putting rocks in the vise grip and busting them open could cause one of us to lose an eye. That's because the topic never came up even though both parents were fully aware of what we were doing in the garage.)

We had other, somewhat safer hobbies, too. Mom made sure that we were both enrolled in figure skating lessons. Every winter, she hauled us to and from practice, and every winter, our skating group had a carnival during which each class performed a song or two. My group did the same routine every year, and after about three years, I got bored of it, but it was good exercise and a fun activity to do with friends. The added bonus was that my Grandma Stuber loved knitting and made us new skating sweaters every year or two. I still have my favourite one—which fit me when I was about six. There's no getting into it anymore but I can't bear to part with it. It has pink, blue, and white stripes in a thick knit that matched beautifully with the white tights I wore for carnival. I was stylin'... and warm!

My favourite hobbies, though, revolved around our horses and music.

My love of music was evident when I was three or four sitting between my mom and dad on the front seat of the car. The automatic gear shift was a stick protruding from the right side of the steering column with a knob at the end of it. When dad was driving, I leaned over and pretended the gear stick and its knob were a microphone, mouthing the words to songs I already knew because the radio was always on. If I didn't know the words, I faked it.

I never sang out loud, though. Nooooooo. My sister was the one who sang around the house, and I was jealous of her confidence to let her voice come out and let others hear it. Until I was a teenager, I only ever lip synced to songs.

I don't know where the desire came from, but I wanted to learn how to play guitar. Maybe it was because most of the music I was surrounded by as a child was what I call old style country music: Tammy Wynette, Merle Haggard, Willie Nelson, and Johnny Cash. A lot of the music Janice and I were exposed to had great guitar rhythms and licks. Something within that music reached inside of me and implanted itself.

I played my first guitar until it broke. When my parents, sister, and I were on our way from Hanna to Fort MacLeod to visit my mom's sister and her family for a weekend, we stopped at the Zellers in Lethbridge. I have no memory of what else my parents bought; I was obsessed with the one thing they bought for me: a toy guitar. It was made of white plastic and it had plastic strings and pictures of Mickey Mouse on the body. It was the perfect size for me and, being as it was a toy, of course it wasn't in tune. I didn't care. It was a guitar! I had wanted a guitar for *so long* (to a four-year old, a few months is a long time), and I finally had one. My parents had to take it away from me on that trip so that I would play with my cousins rather than spend all my time on the guitar, but when we got home, I diverted my full attention to it. We didn't have it long before I broke all the strings and it got tossed into the burning barrel. I was devastated. I felt a massive hole in my tender, young life.

When I was five, my mom enrolled me in private piano lessons with Mrs. Mohl, the elementary school music teacher.

When my parents moved into the new house, they bought my grandparents' piano and moved it into the living room, where it sat for decades until my parents sold the farm. (It's now in my living room.) And my sister, cousins, and I always made a beeline to the organ at my grandparents' house to plunk around, even before we knew how to play. I guess the adults got sick of listening to the random noise because as soon as we acquired the piano, my mom enrolled us in piano lessons.

My mom trucked us into town once a week for our lesson and then enforced the practice rules: We were to practice for half an hour every day. After practicing our lesson material, we were allowed to freestyle on the piano as much as we liked, but the thirty minutes of practice for our lessons was a requirement.

Nut Bags and Num-Nums

My sister quickly became skilled at reading music. I struggled with reading the notes though, and it became evident that I had a knack for playing by ear. Janice didn't have this innate ability. One of the endless ways in which we are opposites.

Because she was older, my sister took her lesson first, and I waited in Mrs. Mohl's living room. Then, it was my turn. The same routine was in place at home: Janice practiced, and I was then sent to the piano bench when she was done.

It only took a few months for Mrs. Mohl and my mother to realize that something sneaky was going on. Yes, I was listening while Janice practiced, and since I could pick up and replicate the music by ear, I did that. It was so much easier than trying to read the notes! When they realized this was my approach, the jig was up. They switched us around so that I had to practice first and take my lesson first. No more cheating.

That's about the time I started to not want to take piano lessons any more. It wasn't that I hated my lessons. I was just lazy and didn't want to read the music. But more than that, I was obsessed with guitar.

Buying me a real guitar was a completely impractical and unreasonable idea. My parents had no money, and we already had the piano. I was to stick with what we had. Plus, there was no one in our town of 2,998 who could offer guitar lessons. It didn't make sense to spend a lot of money on a real guitar if I was only going to hammer away at it and break it like I did with the Micky Mouse guitar without ever learning how to play it.

But I persisted in begging for a real guitar.

Nut Bags and Num-Nums

Janice and I were being brats a couple of weeks before Christmas the year I was eight, and we devised a plan to gang up on our mom and go in search of our Christmas presents. We knew she often bought them early but didn't always wrap them and instead hid them around the house. We were on a mission!

We loudly announced to our mom, "We're going to find our Christmas presents!" and then tore off, each in opposite directions, knowing she could only follow one of us.

Slamming open closet doors, peering behind the couch, sneaking into cubbyholes in the basement. Nuthin, until I ran into my parents' bedroom, flopped myself on the ground on my belly, and peered underneath the bed. Just as I caught a glimpse of something large and black and reached my little hands out to retrieve it, I felt two hands wrap around each of my ankles and hoist me into the air. Mom then stood me up and shoved me out of the room.

I had discovered something!

What was that?

I knew better than to try again. I would get spanked. Besides, I knew my mom would have promptly moved The Large Black Object to a different location, anyway.

Christmas Eve arrived. We are German, so we celebrated Christmas on the twenty-fourth with dinner, church, way too many cookies and candies, and gifts. Our turkey dinner was always on the twenty-fifth, but before going to church for Christmas Eve service, Mom always made something she didn't

139

normally make. Sweet and sour pork ribs were one of the common choices and one that I loved.

That year, as we did every year, we had our dinner and went to church. Then, Dad drove us around town to look at the Christmas lights on people's houses.

***

When your hometown has only 2,998 people, driving through it doesn't take long. I always loved seeing the different decorations, the leadup to stopping at one or both sets of grandparents' houses for a short Christmas Eve visit. My grandmas always had hot chocolate for us and a spread of cookies, cakes, and candies. For some reason, my mom's mom had a tradition of getting halva at Christmastime, as well.

To this day, I have no idea where my grandma's love for this Persian treat originated. We were German. The whole town was white except for two families. Most of the townsfolk had German or other European origins.

What was also curious was that halva was available in the local grocery store at Christmastime. My mom wasn't particularly fond of it, but I loved it and each year, I looked forward to going to Grandma's house on Christmas Eve for so many reasons, including the fact I knew I would get a few bites of halva.

She wasn't alone; her sister Rosie bought it every year, and I know others around town did, too. When I was writing about this tradition, I wondered finally how this treat came to be part of our family Christmas. I asked around.

Nut Bags and Num-Nums

"I don't know," was the common answer I got from a few family members. The only clarification I got was from my uncle Marvin who said, "I guess it was just for the halva of it."

***

As was our tradition, my sister and I changed out of our dresses when we got home from church that night and we then sat down as a family to open gifts. We always took turns so that we could enjoy seeing what each person got.

As we made our way around the circle, I was wondering what the black object I had seen under my parents' bed was. One by one, we opened our gifts, and after the last one had had its wrapping ripped off it, I was puzzled. Nothing that any of us received fit the memory I had of something large, somewhat flat, and black.

We were done. And so Janice and I sat down on the floor to try out the new toys and games we had gotten: new Barbie dolls and accessories, Lite Brite, The Game of Life. (I'm still bitter about the fact that I never *ever* got an Easy Bake Oven when I was a kid though, despite asking for one every year.)

My mom got up and left the room.

When she returned, she was holding The Large Black Object, and she handed it to me.

I immediately knew from the shape what it was.

A guitar case! I flung it open and there, inside, was a brand-new Yamaha acoustic guitar. Not terribly big, but a *real* guitar!

Nut Bags and Num-Nums

I was ecstatic. I sat down and started strumming away on it. Of course it was out of tune, and of course I had no clue what I was doing. But I didn't care.

Hacking away at the out-of-tune guitar only kept me satisfied for so long. I had no idea how to play the thing, and I didn't even know how to tune it so that it sounded not-so-terrible. We had one significant roadblock. We didn't know of anyone in town who could teach me how to play.

I was left frustrated and unsatisfied for three years until we heard there was a new agriculturalist in town who played guitar and who had joined one of the local bands. My mom did some investigating and yes, he was willing and available to teach me to play guitar. One half-hour lesson every Monday for five dollars. I was over the moon.

Until the lessons began.

I didn't know that one big difference between stringed instruments and pianos is that playing any stringed instrument requires building up callouses on the ends of your fingers. And until those callouses are good and hard, playing *hurts*.

But I built up those callouses and dove into my lessons. Yes, this was my instrument. My mom had no trouble getting me to put in my thirty minutes of practice every day. And after my required work was done, I continued to play for another half hour, an hour. Longer. I brought my cassette tape player out of my room and snapped my Eagles cassette into it, playing along with songs like "Take It Easy" and "Peaceful Easy Feeling." Every time we went to Calgary or another town that had a store selling sheet music, I picked up a few selections of songs that were popular at the time: ABBA, Billy Joel, Kenny Rogers. I then taught myself to play these pieces, and sometimes my sister learned them on piano so we could play together.

My dad owned an accordion, which is now in my possession. He was self-taught and was adept at playing old time favourites such as "Beer Barrel Polka" and old hymns. In the winters, when he was less busy with the cattle and had no farming to attend to, he pulled out his accordion on Saturday nights. We spent hours playing together.

My guitar teacher, Lee, was a great instructor: patient, knowledgeable, kind, and funny. I took lessons from him for five years until he moved away. He taught me the art of finger-picking and playing rhythm guitar. Forty years later he still remembers how self-directed I was and that one day, when I showed up for my lesson, I told him I wanted to play something for him before he started my lesson. He sat and listened while I played through "Islands in the Stream", which I had taught myself to finger-pick. Every time I talk to him, he reminds me of how impressed he was that I had done that.

After a couple of years, he deemed that I was good enough to play in public. His band played at dances on Saturday nights now and then at some of the community halls in and around Hanna. For one dance, he arranged with his band to have me join them on stage and play along with "Could I Have This Dance" by Anne Murray. I remember practicing and practicing, not wanting to screw up my big debut and not wanting to make *him* look bad. He had told me to practice it in the key of C, but when he called me up on stage, the band members said they usually played it in G. I panicked.

Nut Bags and Num-Nums

I have only practiced it in C. I can't play it in G.

No matter. For that night, they played it in C.

Lee moved away from Hanna when I was in high school, but with him playing such a significant role in my teenage years, I invited him to attend my high school graduation. He was living up north, and the distance was too great for him to attend. But years later, when I was moving to a new town, I was going through some scrapbooks and piles of stuff I had collected and kept over the years. I found a one-page letter he had written expressing his regret that he couldn't attend my graduation. The majority of the letter contained words of encouragement. He praised me for being a conscientious, well-behaved girl with strong morals, a strong work ethic, and specific goals in life. He talked about how much he admired and respected me, and how he knew I would go on to do exciting things in my life.

We lost touch with each other at some point when I was in my twenties. Then, several years later when I was still teaching high school, I logged into my work email to see a message with the subject line, "I finally found you!" When I saw his name on the sender line, I excitedly opened the message.

I replied immediately, and since then we have remained in touch. We live only a couple of hours away from each other, and the junior hockey teams in his town and mine have the biggest rivalry in the league, so we try to attend hockey games together at least once or twice a year in his town or mine. Now that we are both adults, our relationship is still similar to what it was when I was a teenager except I'm a lot more confident and knowledgeable of the world. And a lot more talkative. He teases me mercilessly, as he did when I was a kid. Our relationship feels

Nut Bags and Num-Nums

like we are uncle and niece. True to his predictions, I did go on to do exciting things and still aim to do so.

***

By the time I was fourteen, something possessed me and my friend Karen to start performing at the senior's lodge in town—both of us singing and me accompanying us on guitar. By then, I had earned my way to an electric guitar and an amp. My mom drove me to town, and Karen and I entertained a room full of local senior citizens with such classics as "Five Foot Two, Eyes of Blue", "You Are My Sunshine", and many more.

Karen asked me to sing at her wedding several years later. Another long-time childhood friend approached me at the wedding reception and said, "I didn't know you could sing!"

I didn't either.

The Lutherans

Karen's dad was one of the many German men in town who did construction work. Phil's Construction was her dad's business. Herb's Construction was my grandpa's. These two men, plus many others, built houses and then, in their later years, worked on smaller construction projects around town. My grandpa was still building garden sheds and dog houses in his early 90s.

Hanna had, and still has, a lot of churches. Because of comments made to me in my younger years, I recall growing up thinking that the Lutherans were "kind of like us" but "those Catholics, Anglicans, and the people from the United Church" were much more relaxed in their beliefs and we were to be cautious that we weren't influenced by them to drink, play cards, or do any other sinful activities.

I was quite confused about religion when I was growing up. My mom's parents were strict: Dancing and playing cards were activities we were not to engage in, yet my parents played cards with their neighbours. My dad drank. My mom drank a little but rarely. We attended community dances every winter, usually once a month, and when I got to junior high school, like my sister before me, I begged to be allowed to go to school dances since all my friends were going.

"Your sister wasn't allowed to go to school dances until grade eight," my mom told me when I asked to go to a grade seven school dance.

"But all my friends are going. Why is it okay to go in grade eight but not grade seven? There's no difference. The dances are the same. Plus, we go to community dances all the time. What's the problem?"

"You're too young to go to a school dance. The community dances are different."

"But what's the difference? It's a DANCE. People are dancing. Just in a different place."

I did manage to convince my mom to allow me to go to *one* dance when I was in grade seven, but Janice and I were instructed to never mention to our grandparents that we went to any dances whether they were school or community dances.

The Bible mentions dancing a lot, so why is dancing sinful?

I never did get satisfactory clarification on that question. Apparently dancing could lead to more sinful activities, but if that was the case, I was still confused about why it was okay for my parents to dance with other people at community dances and why it was okay for me to dance with my parents' friends *as long as I didn't tell my grandparents*.

I was grateful that my Lutheran friends were on the approved list; simply because of their religion and German heritage, they were good influences, even though they drank and danced and played cards. Yup, confusing.

The Lutheran church got a new pastor the summer before I started grade six. His wife and daughters were fun and welcoming, and their adopted daughter, Melanie, was the same age as me. She quickly fit into my circle of friends.

The Lutheran pastor introduced me to Christmas carolling. He organized the youth from his church to go out one evening when Karen, Melanie, and I were in grade seven. We went to the homes of different church members as well as the seniors' manor. The Lutheran church had a bigger youth group than mine did, and so I tagged along with my friends for this outing. The pastor brought his trumpet, and he taught us kids the German words to one verse of "Silent Night". I was thrilled to learn how to sing this, one of my favourite Christmas songs, in the language of my ancestors.

Another of my favourite connections to the Lutheran church was going there every year for pancakes on Shrove Tuesday. Entrance was by donation, and multitudes of people from town and the surrounding towns came out. It was a great social get together with those terrific homemade German sausages.

Headless Criminals and Fried Chicken

I joined 4-H when I was nine or ten. Horses were the main focus of 4-H and of the rodeo club that Janice and I were also in. Our 4-H leaders led us through the "curriculum," teaching us how to properly groom our horses. We had to memorize the parts of a horse, saddle, and bridle. And we learned how to position ourselves and our horses in shows so that the judges could see each part of the horse and evaluate their composition and disposition.

When it came time to travel to shows or rodeos, we often combined our efforts with other families. If one family had room in their horse trailer for another's horses, we horsepooled. And because the kids in each family were similar in age and were friends, sometimes we rode in each other's vehicles.

Our neighbours, Diane and Ernie, often travelled with my family. Diane was one of our 4-H leaders, and their daughter was only a year older than I am, so Janice and I became good friends with her.

The three of us competed in the kids' rodeo in Drumheller. I hopped in to ride to the rodeo grounds with Diane and Ernie. Drumheller's rodeo grounds are a short drive off the highway and are farther down the road from the exit to the medium security penitentiary.

Nut Bags and Num-Nums

As we approached the turn off the highway, Ernie decided to mess with me a bit. I was around ten and was pretty gullible.

"See that big culvert under the approach, Lorna?" he asked

There *was* a culvert connecting both ditches under the approach. It was a lot bigger than most of the culverts near Hanna. At that age, I didn't even know what culverts were for much less why some were bigger than others.

"Yeah," I replied.

"Do you know what they use that culvert for?" he asked me.

"No."

"Well, sometimes the inmates escape from the prison here," he pointed to the penitentiary as we neared the road leading to it. "When the guards or police catch the criminals again, they cut off their heads and throw their heads into the culvert."

Escape? From the penitentiary? Inmates?

The rodeo grounds were so close to the penitentiary.

What are the odds that someone will escape while we are here and come and murder us when we are waiting to compete?

For years after that, I was terrified to look in the direction of the culvert for fear I would see bloody heads piled up inside.

***

Ernie knew my weak spots, and he zeroed in on them.

Nut Bags and Num-Nums

On another trip, I was travelling with my parents, but for the sake of packing the vehicles efficiently, our cooler with our lunch was in Ernie and Diane's vehicle.

Mom usually made fried chicken to take to horse shows and rodeos since it was easy to cook the night before and tasted good cold the next day. Those homegrown chickens with Mom's touch—yum. Since rodeo season was in the summer, the chickens were fresh and tasty after having been butchered in June. One chicken went a long way to feed us and some friends.

We arrived at the rodeo grounds and set ourselves up as we usually did: lawn chairs in front of the arena with a tarp on the ground for our picnic lunch.

We three girls were usually entered in a few events during the day: barrel racing, pole bending, and goat undecorating, which required us to race our horse up to a goat that was tied to a stake driven into the ground in the middle of the arena, dismount, wrap our hands around the rope that the goat was attached to, run along the rope to the goat, and pull a ribbon off of its horn.

When it came time for lunch, all four parents started pulling out the coolers and Ernie targeted me for another of his jokes.

"Oh, Lorna, I know your mom packed fried chicken in your cooler, but we ate it as we were driving here this morning!"

He opened up my mom's cooler and sure enough, no fried chicken. I was too young and naïve to notice that the entire container was gone.

My mom played along with the joke and remained silent.

I had been looking forward to my mom's fried chicken all morning, and having competed in the dust and hot sun, I had worked up quite the appetite. The drumstick was my favourite piece, and since there were two of them, I always got one.

"Your mom's fried chicken is so good, we couldn't help eat it all," Ernie continued. "Here, have a ham sandwich."

He handed me a plate and studied my reaction.

My parents had hammered into us to respect our elders, never talk back, and be obedient. So I glumly but silently took the plate and looked at the container of ham sandwiches he was offering up. I remained silent, but my disappointment couldn't have been more obvious.

As I dished up some potato salad and sulked on the side of the picnic blanket, Ernie eventually felt sorry for me and pulled out the container filled with fried chicken.

I was ecstatic to get my hands on that drumstick.

He teased me about the damn fried chicken for decades, up until he passed away. As I got older and was able to converse with him adult to adult, I teased him back, constantly telling him he owed me a good meal of fried chicken.

***

Mom's fried chicken was also a staple when we went to the Hand Hills Rodeo every June. We got the day of the rodeo off

Nut Bags and Num-Nums

from school every year. Supposedly it was Farmer's Day,[4] but to me, the reason for the holiday was so that we could all attend the rodeo.

We never competed in the rodeo but our family always got together with others to watch it. If the weather agreed, it was a fun way to soak up some vitamin D, enjoy some time with friends or family members, and take in one of our community's most popular pastimes. There were no bleachers, so a lot of people pulled lawn chairs up beside the fence surrounding the rodeo arena. Armed with our pop, snacks (of course Mom's fried chicken for lunch), and the day's program, everyone settled in to enjoy the afternoon's events.

Sometimes my family watched the rodeo with my uncle, aunt, and cousins. Every year, my uncle drove his grain truck to the rodeo grounds, backed it up to the fence, and hosted us or others, who put their lawn chairs in the back of the grain truck for a higher view. He always put a tarp over the grain truck's box so that we had some shade. One year, as we were sitting in the box of his grain truck watching the rodeo, a rainstorm came up and then ended as quickly as it started. The tarp had kept us dry but had also collected the rain. Once the shower had passed, he pushed up on the tarp to get the water off it and in the process, accidently gave the people sitting next to his truck a thorough second shower.

---

4 Farmer's Day used to be the second Friday in June and children in Alberta got the day off of school. The purpose of the holiday was so kids could help on the farm but also to honour the agriculture industry. For more information: coop.ufa.com/news-media/press-releases/history-farmers-day-in-alberta.

Nut Bags and Num-Nums

I said we never competed at the Hand Hills Rodeo. Technically that is correct, but when I was fourteen, my 4-H, rodeo, and school friend Kelly and her younger brother entered the Wild Pony Race. Kelly and I were young teenagers and thought that we were invincible. We had both started helping our fathers with breaking horses at this point, and we thought, *Phhhht. Wild Pony Race. We've got this.* Surely getting on one of those wild *little ponies* was nothing compared to getting on a full-grown unbroken horse, which we had done several times.

The rules for the Wild Pony Race are as follows:

1. Teams of three enter the competition.

2. One team member (the anchor) holds the rope attached to the halter so the pony doesn't get away.

3. A second team member (the mugger) takes the pony's head and as much as possible, covers its eyes, holds the head, does anything (without harming the pony, of course) that can be done to get the pony to stand still ... at least still enough that someone can get on the pony's back.

4. And the third team member is the rider, who is responsible for getting on the pony (bareback—there is no saddle in the mix) and then riding it to, or as close as possible to, the finish line at the other end of the arena.

We hadn't decided who was doing what. We figured we'd wing it once the pony was released from the chute. After all, we were all experienced farm/ranch kids. This would be *so easy*.

Nut Bags and Num-Nums

The three of us held on to the rope, waiting for the event to start. Our pony was in the chute. The other teams were ready, as well. My dad and Kelly's dad were in the arena next to us to coach us along.

TWHEEEEEEEEEEEEEEEEEEEEEEEET

The whistle went, and the chutes flew open.

I felt the jerk on my arms as our pony lurched out of the chute, bucking hard.

"Whoa!" I hollered.

I dug my heels into the dirt and leaned back, trying to hold onto the rope. Kelly pulled back as well, and as we tried to gain control of the pony, her brother fell to the dirt.

He got up, dusted himself off, and looked at us. Kelly and I shook our heads.

"I'm not getting on," Kelly said.

"Me neither!" I replied.

"Come on, you guys. One of you get on," their dad told us.

"I don't wanna, Dad." Kelly's brother's eyes were as big and bright as the full moon, and he had suddenly gone pale in spite of the dirt covering him.

The pony was reared up on its hind legs, pawing at the air with its front hooves.

"Git over there. Git on," my dad instructed me.

"No way!"

Kelly, her brother, and I were unwilling to get closer to the pony. She and I clung to the rope as if our lives depended on it, and her brother remained hunched over beside us. His only movement involved him glancing back and forth between the pony and his dad.

My dad started laughing.

"Yeah, you go ahead and laugh. There's no way I'm getting on that thing!" I hollered at him.

The pony hadn't yet put its front feet on the ground. It was dancing around on its hind legs, towering above us like a demon-possessed horse-shaped UFO hovering in the sky.

"Come on. You guys can do this." Their dad tried again.

Kelly and I ignored him.

Her brother repeated, "I don't wanna, Dad."

Kelly and I stayed in position, both bearing down on the rope. That pony wasn't getting away from us but neither was any of us getting any closer to the wild raging beast.

My dad laughed harder.

The claxon went off, signalling the end of the event. Saved by the horn! I didn't even look to see who, if anyone, had won. I didn't care who won. I cared about the fact that I was still alive.

Nut Bags and Num-Nums

Kelly and I let go of the rope and the five of us walked out of the arena, my dad still laughing and their dad shaking his head. My arms felt two inches longer, my pride two feet shorter.

The Kids'll Be Fine

I saw a meme on Facebook that reminded me of my childhood. The top picture was black and white and depicted several kids and a dog sitting in the bed of a truck. Below it was a picture of three young children wrapped in bubble wrap and seat-belted into the back seat of a car. The top picture was labelled "1975" and the bottom was labelled "today".

I remember when seat belts became law in Alberta. Oh, what a stink in rural Alberta! Never mind that safety was at the heart of the new law; God forbid that The Government tell us what to do! Many of the locals were adamant that they were not going to wear a seat belt.

Until they started getting ticketed for not wearing a seat belt. Several people in my family and circle of friends who shall remain nameless thought they would outsmart the police. They started to pull the seat belt across and snap it in place, but the belt was *behind* their body rather than in front of them. That way, the police would see the belt was pulled across and wouldn't stop them. Except it didn't take long for the police officers to figure out that this is what people were doing. They could tell by the position of the belt that it was behind the person rather than in front of their body. Tickets for all! The Big Bad Government wins again.

Until seat belts became law, we lived in the proverbial Wild West, carefree and heedless of the rules and concerns of today.

Nut Bags and Num-Nums

Our parents and grandparents thought nothing of piling kids, dogs, and adults into the truck bed and driving us from point A to point B. We were never harmed, and we enjoyed the freedom of riding around with the wind blowing through our hair. We quickly learned to hold on to the sides of the truck bed whenever the driver took a turn or hit a bump.

My parents also thought nothing of letting my sister and me tear around on our horses unsupervised, and when we got together with neighbours and their kids, both sets of parents set us free to entertain ourselves, regardless of the season.

The Petersons were one of our closest neighbouring families. Betty and Noel were great friends of my parents, and they had two boys. Irvin was two years older than Janice, his brother Dale was two years younger than she was, and I was two years younger than Dale. Because the boys were older, they often got to choose what we did when we played together so the four of us grew up spending more time playing football and soccer together than playing dolls.

I loved going to the Petersons' place not only because Betty was a great cook (so was my mom, but it was always fun to go to someone else's house for a change of scenery. Betty always made pineapple rice when we came over for supper, something I loved and which my mom almost never made) but roaring around their yard with the boys and their dog was always fun. Plus ... they had a trampoline. I was jealous that they had the trampoline, and every time we went to their farm, I couldn't wait to get on it and continue improving my somersaulting skills. Of course the trampoline wasn't out in the winter; when it was snow season, we found other ways to entertain ourselves building snow forts, going skating on ponds and dugouts that our fathers had cleared for us for this very purpose, and snowmobiling.

Before I was old enough to drive one, I sat behind someone else on the snowmobile, holding on for dear life, loving the thrill of zooming across the prairie on those noisy machines. It was like the winter, motorized equivalent of riding a horse.

When I was old enough, I was allowed to drive a snowmobile myself if there was one for me to drive.

When the Petersons came over to our place to visit for a winter evening, they brought their snowmobiles, so there were four machines: one for each of us kids to drive. The adults were in the house playing cards and visiting while we kids were left to entertain ourselves.

We tore around in the dark, by the light of the moon and the weak headlights on the built-in-the-1970s snowmobiles, racing each other around the farmyard and the pasture just outside our yard. As the youngest, I always had trouble keeping up with the older kids regardless of what we were doing: playing football or soccer, playing tag, riding horses. Roaring around on the snowmobiles was no exception as the older kids were more skilled and braver than I was. Still, I tried to keep up to them.

We had been ripping around for half an hour when we made our way back into the yard. We were still tearing up the snow when I suddenly realized I was approaching a barbed-wire fence, and it was coming at me *fast!*

I'm gonna hit the fence!

Nut Bags and Num-Nums

I panicked but was able to take my finger off the throttle just in time. Feeling my snowmobile slow, I saw the barbed wire of the fence saw through the fiberglass shield in front of me. When my machine stopped, the barbed wire had about an inch to go on the fiberglass before cutting all the way through and then hitting my throat. I had come about a foot away from being decapitated.

Of course I had to explain to my parents why there was a slice in the fiberglass hood of the snowmobile.

"Did you kids have fun snowmobiling?" Mom asked when we came back into the house. They were still playing cards.

"Yeah!" Janice replied. "We went out halfway to the dam and back again. We saw some rabbits and chased them for a while. Then we came back to the yard and Lorna almost drove through the fence."

"What? What happened?" Mom asked me. She put her cards down and turned to look at us.

"Um, well, I couldn't turn or stop in time and my snowmobile hit the fence." I mumbled.

"What happened to the snowmobile and the fence?"

"The fence is okay but it cut through the front of the snowmobile a little. Not all the way." I was still mumbling and shuffling my feet. I wanted to escape the conversation and go downstairs and play.

"Does the snowmobile still work? How much damage is there?"

She got up and looked out the window. It was too dark to see anything except four shadowy shapes of the snowmobiles.

"It's fine. There's just a cut from the barbed wire through the shield in the front but it's not cut all the way through," Janice spoke up for me.

I stared at the floor but I could feel Mom's eyes burning into my little body.

"You need to be more careful. Those machines are expensive, you know."

Even though I was still avoiding eye contact and I knew Mom was directing those words at me, I remained silent.

"You kids can grab a pop from the fridge if you want one to take downstairs," she told us as she sat back down and resumed the card game.

Also, Mom, I ALMOST DIED. Six more inches and that barbed wire would have started cutting through my throat, I thought as I took a grape pop out of the fridge. *But don't worry about me. I'll be fine.*

I followed the other three down to the basement, where we played board games for the rest of the night.

***

Dad and Noel co-owned a bale wagon for several years, sharing the use of it when it came time for retrieving bales from the fields and stacking them on the home property.

Nut Bags and Num-Nums

We used to exchange Christmas gifts with the Petersons,. One of the gifts I remember them giving my parents was a set of two Tammy Wynette 8-track tapes. Of the four of us in my family, I probably spent the most time in front of the stereo listening to music, and so although the tapes were a gift from Betty and Noel to my parents, I played them more than the other three members of my family put together. Today, whenever I hear a Tammy Wynette song, I immediately think of this family of four who were such a huge part of my childhood.

I still exchange Christmas cards with Betty and Noel, even now that my parents have both passed away. They are lifelong friends. And although I haven't seen Irvin and Dale much over the years, I know where they are and I often think of them, these two men who were the closest I had to brothers when I was growing up.

Shitty Pie à la Mode

I've never known a time without horses. Among my earliest memories are moments as a wee tot sitting in front of my dad on his horse, excited and scared but also knowing that I could trust my dad to keep me safe—his strong arm wrapped around me, his hand on my tummy securing my little body between him and the saddle's horn.

When I got old enough to start riding by myself (for a farm kid, this is usually not long after you are potty trained), my first set of training wheels were the four legs of the family's pony, Jill.

Jill was as calm as a glassy lake. She was the perfect horse for kids who wanted to learn how to ride.

Still, sitting high atop a horse was scary for me as a young child. The ground seemed so far below me. The most terrifying experience I had on Jill was when Dad hadn't tightened the cinch quite enough and my saddle swivelled, leaving me hanging below her belly. Jill stood motionless as if having a saddle and a shrieking child dangling below her gut was the most natural thing in the world. In my terrified state, I didn't realize that with my head only inches from the ground, I could have let go and simply crumpled to the ground. Instead, I clung to the saddle horn and squeezed my legs together for dear life, wailing, desperate for one of my parents to come and rescue me from certain death. My young brain knew that this predicament had grave potential. Thank goodness for a docile animal.

Nut Bags and Num-Nums

A few years later when I levelled up to Freddie, I was old enough to be ready for adventure and speed. Freddie, like most of my clothes, was a hand-me-down from my sister, and like those clothes, served me well until I too outgrew him.

Freddie was a short and stocky horse. He was the equine equivalent of a bouncing, happy, pudgy dog, greeting its owner coming home from work. We could tell he loved us as much as we loved him. If horses could smile, he would have worn a permanent grin.

He was Janice's favourite horse.

"I remember so well when Dad bought him at the Hanna Auction Market. I wanted that horse so bad. The bidding kept increasing and Dad kept bidding. He bought Freddie for $260, and I was so afraid our parents couldn't afford that," she says. "These days, you can't even get out of Costco for $260."

But our parents were committed to supporting our involvement with horses. Plus, Janice and I each needed a reliable horse so we could help Dad with the cattle. Janice got her Freddie. When she got too big for him, he was mine.

My sister had started barrel racing with him and then she graduated to a fancy schmancy barrel horse a neighbour had found in Texas and brought back to Canada for our family. I then picked up the reins and began to barrel race Freddie at the local amateur rodeos. I don't recall anyone formally training him to run the clover-leaf pattern, but he did his job well and never balked. We won a bit of prize money now and then.

Nut Bags and Num-Nums

After Dad bought Janice her fancy barrel horse, Freddie and I had a hard time keeping up with her. I was still on the cusp of being able to completely control my horse—some days I could and others I couldn't. I was young, a bit inexperienced, and not as strong as one should be to fully control a horse. There was therefore a lot of trust involved for all—horse and human alike.

My sister and I often went riding in the pasture together for fun. We were moseying along on the dusty prairie when Janice decided it was time to break out into a full gallop. Without warning, she suddenly took off ahead of me. Of course I wanted to keep up, and even more than that, Freddie did. He took off at full tilt.

I resigned myself to the fact that I was going to have to sit tight until Janice decided to slow down, which would then prompt Freddie to slow down. I held on for dear life and focused on just staying mounted.

I would have been fine except Freddie tripped in a gopher hole. My last memory was seeing his shoulder and the ground blasting toward me. I don't remember hitting the ground.

I *had* hit the ground. And *hard*. I was out cold for close to probably fifteen minutes—the time it would have taken for my sister to race back to the house, about a quarter of a mile away, tell my parents that I was seemingly dead on the prairie, and get them to come with the truck and retrieve my corpse.

I woke up seated between my dad, who was driving, and my mom, in the passenger seat. We were in the red and white pickup truck, driving back to the house. I was only awake for a few seconds.

Nut Bags and Num-Nums

I next awoke in my bed. I had no idea how much time had passed between my waking in the truck and waking this time. I was comfy and safe in my bed. No broken bones, no blood. But I had the worst taste in my mouth. I had taken a good-sized bite out of a cow pie (every other kind of pie tastes *so* much better!) when I hit the ground, and cow manure was firmly lodged between my teeth. I got up and rinsed my mouth out, but I could still taste the manure and I could still feel grit in my teeth. I went back to bed.

If you apply today's line of thinking to this incident, this would already be well past the point at which my parents would have taken me to the hospital to get me checked out.

Nope. This was the late 1970s, and I was a farmer and rancher's daughter. Even though I had obviously hit my head hard enough to be rendered unconscious, my good ol' parents put me to bed so I could *sleep ... it ... off.*

Oh wait ... it gets better.

We were scheduled to go to the Petersons' that night for dinner. And so when it came time to leave, Mom pulled me out of bed, and off to the neighbours' we went. Over dinner, Mom told the Petersons about my little accident.

"Oh my gosh! Thank goodness you are okay! More pineapple rice?"

"Yes, please. Thank you, Betty."

My appetite was unaffected, which turned out to be unfortunate because the vanilla ice cream I had for dessert had the distinct flavour of cow pie. Any *other* kind of pie goes well with ice cream.

My mom never did take me to the doctor to get checked out.

Perhaps that's because accidents with horses were commonplace on the farm. Even expected. And what was also expected was that you just "dust yourself off and get back on again." The cowboy motto.

When I was a few years older, I had another horse overlapping with Freddie. Her name was Cheri, and I rode her for a couple of years before Dad decided to use her for breeding. She gave birth to several foals year after year, and one of them was a bay filly that I claimed as my own. Her name was Cosita. I was going to break her, and she was going to be mine.

But *she* hadn't signed up for that. When she was old enough to start taking the saddle, I eased her in, putting the saddle on her and leading her around the yard for a few days before I tried riding her. Of course, the first time I mounted her, I promptly landed face first in the dirt. But *you get up, dust yourself off, and get back on again.*

After a few short rides around the yard without incident, it came time to go for a longer ride on Cosita. Dad and I set out on our respective mounts and headed into the pasture. We got an eighth of a mile from home when a bird flying out of the brush spooked my young horse and she exploded into a bucking frenzy. She launched me off her and I landed on my belly *hard*, the wind knocked out of me.

Nut Bags and Num-Nums

As I lay on the ground gasping for air, "HHHHHHHHHHHHHHUUUUUUUUUUU," thinking I was surely dying, Dad silently got off his horse and held Cosita's reins so she wouldn't take off. Funny, as soon as she ejected me, she stood perfectly still. She, my dad, and his horse stood patiently waiting for me to get back on my feet.

There isn't much you can do for someone when they get the wind knocked out of them. Nor can you do anything for yourself except wait for your body to recover. When I could breathe normally again, I stood up, *dusted myself off, and got back on* while Dad held her. We headed back to the farmyard. Clearly that was enough for me and Cosita that day.

When we got back, we unsaddled and turned the horses into the corral. Dad went about his business working with other animals and I went into the house to get a bit of a proper rest. My brain cells were still rattling around as if my skull were a pinball machine.

Come suppertime, the four of us gathered at the table. My dad was dying to tell my mom and sister about my spectacular fall off my horse.

"All of a sudden Cosita started bucking like crazy. Lorna landed smack dab on the ground. And she was lying there trying to breath... HHHHHHHUUUUU HUUUUUUUU..."

And he let out his deep belly laugh.

"It wasn't funny!" I said.

But I couldn't help laughing, too.

Nut Bags and Num-Nums

I got precisely zero sympathy from Dad, Mom, and Janice for that incident, as well. Getting bucked off a horse is just a fact of life on the farm.

Once I got too big for Freddie, my parents went looking for a suitable long-term horse for me since Cheri was now a breeding mare. My sister continued improving her barrel racing times, and I had to decide: Did I want to focus on barrel racing, or did I simply want a reliable horse that I could show and use to help my dad with cattle ranching? I chose the latter.

I felt that my new horse, Dawn View Cinders (we called him Cinders), launched me into an even more prestigious category as he was half Quarter Horse and half Arabian. He was registered with the Arabian association.

I was excited to have a horse whose breeding brought me into the world of Alec Ramsay from The Black Stallion books that I loved so much when I was younger.

Except Cinders was obnoxious.

I loved him deeply, just as I loved all our other pets and farmyard animals, but it seemed Cinders wasn't terribly enamoured of me. The trick to catching a horse when they are in the pasture or corral is to take a bucket of oats, shake it, call their name, and halter them when they come running. They get to eat the oats as a reward for behaving well. Cinders always ran the other way. He seemed to hate me enough to deny himself the treat. I always eventually caught him, but he didn't make it easy.

Nut Bags and Num-Nums

But he was a damn good horse once I had my hands and legs on him.

Cinders' previous owner told us that she had started to train him to do some show jumping.

I had only ever ridden in a Western saddle, so after we acquired Cinders, my parents bought me an English-style saddle, bridle, and the whole getup—jodhpurs, helmet, jacket, and boots—so that I could learn to ride English-style and try my hand at jumping Cinders in some shows. My devoted father built some jumps for me to practice with at home, so Cinders and I prepared for and entered some amateur competitions.

My show jumping career was short-lived. As much as I loved jumping, Cinders grew increasingly unpredictable, coming to a sudden halt in front of random jumps without warning during competitions. After several tumbles over his shoulder, I gave up on competing thinking, *I'm gonna quit while I HAVE a head. One of these times I'm going to fall and break my neck.*

I then discovered by accident that Cinders had a secret, useful talent.

On one of the countless days of my youth when I was out in the field helping my dad move cattle, a couple of cows strayed from the main herd. I was closest to them, so I signalled to Cinders to turn and move toward the cows. We loped over to where they were and guided them back to the herd. Moments later, when another cow tried to break from the herd, Cinders went after the cow without any prompting from me, and he pushed her back into place. Something clicked in my brain.

Nut Bags and Num-Nums

This horse has been trained to cut cattle!

From that point on, I became one of the designated riders to cut cattle from the herd. Cinders was the only horse we owned who had natural cutting skills, and he seemed to love doing it.

One of Cinders' quirks that amused me was his impatience with the baby calves. When we were herding cows with their calves, of course the calves would dawdle and play around, as babies of any species do. If they were lagging behind, once he finally had enough of their antics, he would lower his head and bite them on their bums to get them moving.

***

When I was entering my teens, my dad bought a team of heavy horses. Duke and Scotty were beautiful blond Belgians, around three years old when we acquired them. They were gentle, kid-friendly, and reliable. In the winters, Dad hitched them up to a hay wagon and used them to take hay out to the cattle in the pasture, and in the summers, he entered them and the hay wagon in the Hanna parade. I fell deeply in love with these gentle giants, and although I couldn't do much with them—I wasn't strong enough to drive them and of course, we didn't ride them since they were heavies—I often went out to the corral to pet them and talk to them.

An extra treat from my dad came in the winters when we had Duke and Scotty. My mom encouraged my sister and me to invite our friends over for hayrides. Dad loved driving his team, and they were the perfect team to take a group of rowdy kids out for a winter evening ride. The rides always ended with hot chocolate in the house or around a fire outside. If we had a fire in the yard, of course we roasted marshmallows.

I like my roasted marshmallows a nice golden brown; I hate it when they burn, so when one of my marshmallows caught fire, I instinctively started waving my stick back and forth to try and wave the fire way. The fire dissipated, but in the process, the gooey marshmallow went flying and landed *splat* on the front of Janice's brand-new winter jacket.

***

When I moved away from the farm to attend university, I left Cinders behind with my parents. I rode him any time I was home, but by the time I was twenty, no one else was using him much as my dad had his own horses, and it was too hard for me to make the six-hour round-trip drive home. Cinders was a few years older than I was—a senior citizen in horse years—and so it was time to sell him.

I've not had my own horse since. I long to live on a farm again, with access to wide-open prairie or rolling foothills. I'd love to have a horse I could hop on and ride for enjoyment any time I desire. It was my greatest source of pleasure when I was a kid. I miss the freedom and the unity one feels with an animal that saunters in any direction you direct it.

In the past thirty-plus years, however, I've taken any opportunity I could to go riding. When I was working at an ESL school in Calgary, we occasionally took our international students on horseback rides for summer excursions. When my friend from Germany came to visit and brought along her Irish husband, who wanted the full Billy Crystal *City Slickers* experience, my dad scouted out a great place in the Rockies near Sundre for the four of us to go for a day-long ride.

And I jumped at the chance to ride an Arabian horse along the shore of the Red Sea when I was in Egypt in November 2019. My afternoon ride in the Egyptian desert took me back to my early memories of reading Farley's stories of The Black Stallion. In Hurghada, Egypt, enjoying an exhilarating ride in the Egyptian desert sand, I created my own Alec Ramsey story.

I got up close and personal in Las Vegas several years ago with Wayne Newton's beautiful Arabian horses. A friend and I took a tour of Newton's estate, Casa de Shenandoah. Part of the property contains a horse pasture, and several of his horses were frolicking about the day we were there. I ignored the signs stating that we were not to touch the horses.

Bah, I know what I'm doing around horses, I thought. And as I reached out to stroke his velvet muzzle, the Arabian treasure bit me. Served me right!

My equine memories jostled me again as I rode over volcanic rock along the beach in southern Iceland in May 2022. A friend and I were on a three-day horseback riding tour southeast of Reykjavik. As my stocky little Icelandic mount and I tölted[5] along the riding paths, I mulled over a skill I have possessed all

---

[5] Icelandic horses have four gaits; some have five. The fourth gait, the tölt, is similar to a trot but unlike a trot, the horse has only one leg on the ground at a time. This gait, which only Icelandic horses possess, is smooth, comfortable, and fast. A horse in the tölt gait looks (and feels) almost like it is floating.

my life—the ability to confidently handle (almost) any horse upon my first encounter with them.

My riding ability has opened up some incredible opportunities for me. Along with the experiences above, I've ridden a mule to the bottom of the Grand Canyon (and back to the top), an elephant in Thailand, and a camel in Egypt. Not to say that riding a camel through a Nubian village along the shores of the Nile is anything like riding a horse on the Canadian prairie, but being comfortable hopping on the back of a large four-legged creature allows me to easily embrace and enjoy unique adventures that many others might be afraid to try.

All Thumbs

In addition to my probable concussion when I flew over Freddie's shoulder, I've had other accidents. Another time a horse bucked me off in the middle of our yard, I again hit the ground stomach first. One of the horse's hooves landed on my lower back as she was jumping. I was in excruciating pain for days afterward, and so I got Mom to take me to the doctor. X-rays revealed I had some fractured ribs, and there was nothing the doctor could do about them. I just had to tough it out. As the doctor was examining me, he commented on the pristine horseshoe-shaped bruise on my lower back which, over the first week after the accident, turned beautiful shades of black, blue, green, and yellow.

When I was in elementary school, Mom told me about a neighbour who, years before I came along, had lost his leg after getting it caught in the grain auger. After hearing that story, I was always extra cautious when working around the auger and other farm machinery.

In my elementary school years, I was horrified to hear about an accident one of our neighbours had. Several of the neighbours took part in team roping competitions as an extension of their working cowboy duties, and on one occasion, this neighbour's thumb got caught up in the lariat when he threw it to rope the steer. The good news was he caught the steer. The bad news was, the steer continued running at full speed while the rope tightened around our neighbour's thumb.

Nut Bags and Num-Nums

Thumbs are no match for a one-thousand-pound animal running at near full speed, and so his glove, caught up in the rope, followed the steer, thumb included. Yeow! I can't imagine how painful that would have been.

Even though my grandpa had retired from farming, he kept himself busy well into his nineties doing construction jobs. I was thankfully not witness to this mishap but on one occasion when he was using a table saw, he got his hand a little too close to the blade and cut the end of his thumb off around the first joint. He took the end of his thumb home, where Grandma promptly plopped it into a plastic bag and put it into the freezer until Grandpa was able to go the doctor to see if they could reattach it. By the time he "got around" to going to the doctor, it was too late to reattach the tissue. He kept on doing building projects for the next thirty some years with a stub where his full thumb used to be.

I was always careful around machinery, but when you are dealing with animals, you can take all the precautions in the world and still get hurt because as tame as they may seem, animals are still that and can be unpredictable at times.

I was less cautious when I was eleven and Janice and her boyfriend at the time took me roller skating in town. It was the early 1980s and someone in town got the idea of opening up the skating rink in the summer so people could go roller skating. With my background in figure skating, I wasn't at all hesitant to put on the roller skates, and I did pretty well until on our third time going, I was overconfident when "shooting the duck." My feet swept out from under me, and my butt smacked down onto the cement. I was in extreme pain for the next several days.

Nut Bags and Num-Nums

After the pain hadn't subsided several days in, I got my mom to take me to the doctor, who ordered X-rays. The X-rays revealed I had a fractured tailbone and, guess what? You can't cast a tailbone. Again, I could only wait it out. The doctor did have one solution to offer, although he didn't guarantee it would work. An injection which, in *hindsight* (ba-dum-tiss), I suspect was likely cortisone. Yep, he pulled out a needle about a foot long, instructed me to pull down my pants and bend over, and inserted the needle upward along my butt crack. So fun.

But the next day, and every day forward, I miraculously had no pain in my butt. Still now—no pain!

When I was in my mid-twenties, one day my back seized up with no warning and for no reason. I went to the doctor. Apparently I had an arthritis flareup in the muscle that the horse had stepped on. The horseshoe-shaped bruise was long since gone; there was no visible scarring on my skin, but this pain rattled me.

I'm twenty-five! And I'm having problems with arthritis because of this injury? Is this the beginning of dealing with constant back pain for the rest of my life? I'm too young for this!

The doctor prescribed anti-inflammatories, which released the pain. In a few days I felt fine again, and I haven't had problems with that muscle since.

I do wonder, as I get older, how some of these injuries will come back to haunt me when I get into my sixties and seventies. Ah well, it was all worth it. At least I can say that now ....

I Found My Voice

As I moved from elementary to junior high school, I kept busy with my horses but I also developed new interests, most of which I was introduced to in school. I've never been athletic, but in grade seven I liked soccer and thought I could maybe be good at it. I asked Mom if I could join the school soccer team, but she wouldn't let me. Practices were at 7:00am, and that was too early for her to take me to town. We had to do morning chores.

Acting in church Christmas pageants and plays had sparked my interest in acting on stage. Drama was one of the options we could take in junior high school. I chose it each of the three years.

Our Drama teacher was also my Math teacher for grade eight. He was an easygoing, fun-loving man with a fabulous head of curly 1980s hair, and we all liked him because he was so good-natured. One day in Math class when he was writing on the blackboard, my classmate Blake, who was sitting in the front seat, turned around to face the class, made a circle with the thumb and forefinger of one hand and pushed the index finger of his other hand in and out, making a sexual innuendo. Our teacher turned around and asked, "Blake, what are you doing?" We all burst out laughing as Blake's face reddened. He turned around and got back to work.

Our teacher was equally as laid back in Drama class and gave us fun projects including making music videos. He had us choose a group to work with, choose a song, and create a video to accompany it. He used the video camera to record all of our videos and showed them to the class so we could see one another's creations. Since this was in the early days of MTV, we were all excited to be emulating our favourite singers and groups by making music videos, which were all the rage at that time. One of the videos my group made was to the song "Physical" by Olivia Newton John. We dressed up in our gym clothes, took some floor mats from the gym, and did a series of somersaults, jumping jacks, and other exercises while the song played. It was a pretty clean, junior high school, totally off-the-mark interpretation of the song.

When I got to high school, Drama wasn't an option, so I chose other classes such as Typing, Computers, and Accounting. But one of our new high school teachers had a strong background in performing arts—drama and dance in particular. He started a drama club, gathering those who were interested and organizing a production of a full play. He cast all of the roles and also put students in charge of the production side. My role in the first play he produced was stage manager. For some reason, I opted to take part behind the scenes even though up to that point I had had a lot of experience acting in church plays and in junior high Drama class. I guess I wanted to try something new. I was in my element. I found that I liked being behind the scenes much more than I enjoyed acting. The one aspect of acting that I always found terrifying was worrying that I would forget my lines. I'm good at organizing, delegating, and prioritizing, so stage management was a natural fit for me.

The following year, he and one of the junior high teachers arranged for both schools to put on a production of the play *Bye*

Nut Bags and Num-Nums

Bye Birdie. I wanted to be stage manager, but I didn't step forward to assert myself for the role. He and the other teacher chose someone else so I looked for other ways to be involved. The play is a musical—the story of a young rock singer who is drafted into the US army and performs a farewell concert before going overseas to serve. The music is typical 50s and 60s style, and so it's fun to play on guitar. The orchestra for our production needed a guitar player. Bingo!

I joined the orchestra along with several men from around town. When it came time to rehearse with the cast, we set up in the school gym. Our orchestra pit was a small, enclosed area that had been walled off with temporary partitions. In our first rehearsal, I burst out laughing during one of the jokes in the script, only to be met with disapproval by the female teacher who was leading the production with our teacher.

"The ONLY sound coming from the orchestra pit is to be music!" she hollered.

From that point on, I muffled my laughter.

That was the last big production our junior and senior high schools did together when I was living in Hanna. However, Stage Hanna was and still is part of the larger community, putting on shows each year.

***

In addition to learning the parts of the horse, saddle, and bridle, each member of our 4-H club had to record in official record books how we cared for our horses—what we fed them, how often we dewormed them and trimmed their hooves (Dad did that task), and how often we rode them. I loved filling out the pages of my record book, detailing what I was learning and how I spent my time with my horse.

But the one requirement of 4-H that I dreaded in my first year was the public speaking competition. By the time I joined 4-H, I had starting to talk to some of my classmates more and had only timidly and rarely begun to raise my hand in class to answer questions.

Make a five-minute speech at the front of the room in front of all the other 4-H members and their parents? And in front of JUDGES? I'd rather be in the bathtub with Jaws snacking on me!

The public speaking component was a judged competition. We got to choose the topic of our speech, but every member had to take part. No exemptions.

Choosing my topic that first year was easy.

"Hey Mom, you know Terry Fox is running across Canada to raise money for cancer?"

"Yes?"

"I thought maybe my 4-H speech could be about him. You know, how he found out he got cancer, and his operation, and why he's running across Canada. About how he's running a marathon every day on one leg!"

"That's a good idea. It's a good topic."

"Yeah, I can look through all of the Maclean's magazines and find lots of information about him in those articles and in other magazines and newspapers. And I can read about cancer in the encyclopedia. It'll be easy to find lots of information."

That Mom kept every magazine she had ever subscribed to was a huge benefit to me at that time. She had gotten a subscription to Maclean's when Janice entered junior high school, thinking it would be a good source of information for both of us as we worked through our junior and senior high school years.

I pulled a stack of magazines off the shelf in Mom's office and started flipping through them for any information I could find about Terry Fox and about cancer. My interest in my topic quickly overshadowed the dread I initially felt when thinking about getting up and speaking to a roomful of other humans.

I spent the next few days jotting notes and organizing the information before writing a draft of my speech.

"Here, Mom, how is this?"

I handed her a few pages of loose leaf.

"I think you can take out this sentence and maybe this paragraph," she told me. "Maybe move this part to here."

After a few edits, my speech was ready. I carefully copied it onto the recipe cards I would use while presenting the speech.

And then I practiced.

"Slow down a little bit," Mom advised. "If you talk too fast, people won't be able to understand you."

I focused on speaking a bit more slowly.

"Look up more, The judges are going to look for how much eye contact you make with the audience."

The more I practiced, the more familiar I became with the speech. I made mental notes of places where I could look up and make eye contact with the judges and audience without losing track of where I was.

By the day of the competition, I was confident and ready to attempt this scary deed.

"On April 12, 1980, Terry Fox dipped his artificial leg into the Atlantic Ocean in St. John's Newfoundland and began his Marathon of Hope."

The girl who had always been terrified of making eye contact and speaking to strangers stood in front of around thirty other 4-H members and their parents, as well as three judges, and told the story of how a young man from BC who had had his leg amputated due to cancer was dedicating his time and energy to running across Canada, twenty-six miles per day, to raise money and awareness for cancer research.

"His goal is to raise twenty-four million dollars—one dollar for every Canadian."

In my mind and in my speech, he was a selfless example of a Canadian hero.

I made eye contact with the audience, I looked and smiled at the judges, I spoke slowly, varying my intonation. And I used facial and hand gestures to emphasize my main points.

Whew. Well, that's over with. I don't have to do this again for another year, I thought as I sat down.

After everyone finished their speeches, one of the judges went to the front of the room to announce the winners.

"And the winner of the junior category is Lorna Stuber."

What? Me?

I got up to receive my plaque. Everyone was clapping, and I was stunned.

I won? Me? I guess I did pretty well!

"All of the first, second, and third place winners will be going on to Regionals, which will be held in Acadia Valley in three weeks," the judge continued. "You will use the same speech, and you will be competing against the winners from the other 4-H clubs in this area. We will phone all of you next week with the details."

Regionals? I won, and the "reward" is that I have to do this all over again but in a ROOMFUL OF COMPLETE STRANGERS?

The fear was fleeting, though. Winning the competition at the local level hiked my confidence for speaking to a level it had never been at before.

Why am I so terrified of speaking to other people if I can win a speaking competition? Obviously I'm good at this. Maybe speaking up isn't so scary, after all.

Nut Bags and Num-Nums

I placed second at Regionals, only coming behind a boy from Acadia Valley. He and I then moved on to Provincials, and again, I came in second to him.

***

I've always thought it was ironic that a kid who was so terrified of speaking to anyone other than her parents and sister for the first ten years of her life shone in a public speaking competition and even enjoyed public speaking and acting on stage. My comfort and confidence in these situations paved the way for me to enjoy the time I spent speaking to a room full of students after I became a teacher. I still much prefer public speaking to engaging in small talk with strangers or trying to join a group conversation at a social gathering. Maybe the idea of being a subject-matter expert and talking to people about my knowledge rather than more personal matters is what makes the difference.

The Hallowed Weenies

As I was learning to speak up more confidently, I was also having to come to terms with some elements of my childhood that were ending.

Halloween is such an odd occasion. It's the one day of the year when any of us who aren't film or stage actors can adopt a completely different character for a day and act as such without any excuses, explanations, or embarrassment. A character of our choosing. And it's the one day when we actively encourage kids to go against the whole "don't take candy from strangers" warning that we hammer into them the other 364 days of the year. Weird stuff.

But I guess weirdness is the whole point of Halloween. It is, after all, the day intended to scare evil spirits away. I can't speak for the evil spirits, but I like weirdness, so if I were an evil spirit, Halloween wouldn't be terribly effective at keeping me at bay. It would just egg me on.

Yes, I love Halloween, maybe *because* I love weirdness.

Take, for example, the time when, in junior high, my friend Kelly and I were out trick-or-treating with her brother (who was still young enough to go trick-or-treating—Kelly and I were old enough that we were pushing it). The two most memorable stops that night included the home of someone we didn't know, which was rare in a town the size of Hanna. Some guy opened his door, beer in hand, cigarette in his mouth, hairy belly hanging out of the bottom of his white tank top, and promptly called us out.

"Aren't you girls a little old to be trick-or-treating? You wanna beer?"

We thanked him for the offer but declined and left with chocolate bars instead.

We also made a point of stopping at many of our teachers' homes each year, and the second incident happened during such a stop. When Mr. Ghidina, our fun-loving Science teacher, answered his door, Kelly and I immediately opened up our pillowcases, showing him the aerosol cans of shaving cream at the bottom, and confessed that we had every intention of writing on his car, which was parked on the street behind us. He plopped some candy into our bags, said, "Okay." He leaned against his doorframe while we trekked to his car, pulled our ammunition out of our pillowcases, and followed his instructions. Yes, he told us exactly what he wanted us to write on his car: "#1 Teacher". We were quite happy to write that because in our minds, he was.

After we had done the deed, we thanked him, waved at him (he waved back), and continued with our evening.

Weird.

Growing up on a farm ten minutes outside of a small town meant that Janice and I needed parental assistance for trick-or-treating. Sometimes we stayed in town after school, hung out at one of our sets of grandparents' homes, and started out from

Nut Bags and Num-Nums

there. Other years, we went home and Mom brought us back into town. The farms were too far apart to bother going to, although someone failed to tell that to one of our neighbours one year when the four of us woke on November 1st to find that we couldn't get out of the house. During the night, someone had felt it necessary to take several straw bales from my dad's bale stacks and build a wall against the door, completely trapping us. We never did find out who pulled that prank.

There's a good chance that whoever stacked the bales against our door was one of the neighbours who attended the local community dances in the fall and winter, so it's quite likely that Mom and I got revenge on that person indirectly a few years after they had imprisoned us. I was in grade seven when the movie *E. T. the Extra-Terrestrial* came out, and the following year, Mom sewed me an E. T. costume. It's a head-to-toe costume (I still have it) complete with gloves, and there's no way to know who is inside unless you know with 100 per cent certainty whose eyes you are looking at. I wore the costume to school for our Halloween party, and I also wore it in town for trick-or-treating. The community Halloween dance was a few days after Halloween, and anyone who was at the dance wouldn't have seen the costume yet. My parents and I devised a plan that we thought would be funny.

Mom and I went to the dance in her car, arriving right around the time that it started, and Dad came separately in his truck ... wearing the E. T. costume. Mom and I told everyone that Dad couldn't come to the dance because he was tending to a sick cow but Mom had brought me because I really wanted to attend. We thought this was completely plausible, as everyone knew I liked attending the dances. She and I had been there about ten minutes when E. T. walked in the door solo and set the place abuzz. Pretty much everyone else was recognizable in their costumes, and so people were completely mystified as to who was in this costume.

E. T. promptly walked over to the wife of one of the other farmers in our area, put out his hand, and silently led her to the dance floor. They circled the floor for the whole song, and by the look on the poor woman's face, she clearly had no clue who she was dancing with and was also a little unnerved at the whole situation. Mom and I had a hard time trying not give the secret away by laughing too hard.

The tricks are fun, but Halloween is *all* about the treats. And we were treated well in our small town. My grandparents always made special treat bags for me and my sister—the ubiquitous brown lunch bags filled with homemade cookies, popcorn balls, and wads of candy instead of just one or two mini chocolate bars that they would give every other kid. My aunt Rosie did the same, and so did Irvin and Dale's grandparents. We always knew that when we knocked on so-and-so's door, they would shuffle off to the side and grab one of the special bags that they had ready for us.

We also quickly learned who gave out the best stuff in general, and we made sure they were high on our list year after year. In the 1970s and 80s, there were no chain businesses in my hometown. Instead of a 7-Eleven convenience store, we had a small family-owned convenience store called 10-11 ... which the whole town referred to as The Ten to Eleven because they were open from 10:00am to 11:00pm ... which meant they were open during trick-or-treating hours. We made sure went there

Nut Bags and Num-Nums

every year because they were the only place in town that gave out full-sized chocolate bars, and they always let us pick our own off the shelf.

Half a block from 10-11 was the town's butcher shop—Central Meats—which everyone called The Meat Market. And so yes, it was an actual meat market, not a sleazy bar. Coincidently, the sleazy meat-market-type bar (the one bar in town that had strippers) was kitty-corner from the meat market. One year, as my sister and I were leaving the 10-11, we noticed the lights of Central Meats were on. Everybody in town knew the owners, and as anyone who grew up in a small community knows, trick-or-treating isn't just about getting candy. It's also about socializing—getting a chance to chat with people you may not have seen for a while. So we stopped at the meat market to say hi and see what they had to offer. They obviously hadn't expected any trick-or-treaters; they didn't have any candy on hand. Not wanting to send us away empty-handed though, the owner was quick on his feet. He pulled out of the display case a couple of the individually wrapped bulk wieners found in the meat section of any grocery store and plopped one into each of our bags.

Raw weenies! I was over the moon. I mean, we expected full-sized chocolate bars from the convenience store and popcorn balls from our grandparents and friends' grandparents, but this was the ultimate prize. *I love eating raw wieners*, still to this day. Yeah, I know, I know ... let's not even talk about what wieners are made of ("Lips and assholes," according to Janice) but I do indulge in a good hot dog at a hockey game once a year or so. And though I haven't done so in years, it wouldn't take much to convince me to grab a raw wiener from the fridge and have it for an afternoon snack. The next day at school, my friends, of course, thought our haul at the meat market was hilarious, and I'm pretty sure they were also all jealous that none of them had thought to stop there.

It occurred to me as I was writing this that, if, at the age of fourteen, I was offered a beer when trick-or-treating, and shouting "Halloween apples, trick-or-treat!" at the meat market got us raw wieners, I really should have gone trick-or treating the year I turned sixteen and stopped at the car dealership.

Welcome, Friend. Goodbye, Friend

When there are fewer than two hundred kids in your entire school, you see the same kids all day every day of the school year, year after year. So when a family moves to town with a kid who joins your class, the new kid is a novelty and those of you who have known each other for years clamour all over one another, sussing out the new kid to see where they fit. It's like a job interview for the new kid. Which group do they fit into and who will claim them? Sometimes it's a bit of a tug-of-war. Other times it happens quickly and naturally.

Jay moved to town with his mom and dad at the beginning of our grade nine year. We met in Reading class. Yes, when I was in junior high school, Reading was one of the options we got to choose from. Of course it wasn't to teach us how to read. But it was a kind of extension of Language Arts class. We had a list of books to choose from and during each class, we sat in our desks ... reading. And then we wrote book reports about the books we read. Other than Music class, which, after the chicken salad debacle, I didn't choose in junior high school, Reading was the option best suited to me.

Jay and I bonded over our love of reading. And he slid easily into my group of friends.

We also quickly discovered he and I had a common obsession: ancient Egypt. I remembered learning about Egypt's pharaohs in grade six, and he must have as well. As fourteen-year-olds, we made a pact that we would go to Egypt together someday. Being the idealistic kids that we were, we figured it would never happen what with Egypt being so far away, but the year we turned fifty, we made it happen. "Someday is today," he said to me as our plane departed from Calgary in November 2019.

Along with a new friend, my grade nine year brought to me the loss of my innocence. During those first fourteen years of my life, my parents had attended several funerals, and so I knew that death and the ceremony that followed it was a natural part of life. But when I was fourteen, I started attending funerals. And they came hard and fast that year.

My great-grandpa died at ninety-six, but his death was not a shock to me. He was an old man.

Death hits harder when it comes calling for someone who does not die of "old age".

On the last day of school before Christmas vacation in grade nine, students from all three grades, along with our teachers, went outside for a skating and toboggan party. As much as I loved both of these activities, I opted to stay back in the school. I had two friends who weren't able to take part: Melanie, the adopted daughter of the Lutheran pastor in town, had a medical condition that I didn't know the name of. Based on what I know now, I suspect she had *Osteogengesis imperfect*, also known as "brittle bone disease." This is a genetic condition with symptoms such as the ones Melanie had: easily broken bones, bowing of the legs and other bone deformities, a curved spine, and a barrel-

Nut Bags and Num-Nums

shaped chest.[6] She was also quite short—at least a good foot shorter than the rest of us. Because her bones broke easily and because of her weakened muscles and bowed legs, she walked with a walker. She couldn't take part in a lot of activities, such as the skating party that last day of school before Christmas break. Definitely no tobogganing for someone who broke a rib sometimes just from sneezing!

Another friend, Carrie, also stayed back. She had such severe asthma that she was often exempt from physical education class because the exertion could send her into a potentially dangerous, extreme asthma attack. Those two girls, plus me and a couple others, stayed back to play board and card games while our other classmates frolicked outside.

When everyone came back, we had a pizza party. By the time we finished licking our fingers, it was time for us farm kids to board the school busses and go home. We wished each other a Merry Christmas and dispersed to our respective busses. Carrie said goodbye to me as she walked to her bus.

Two days later, I was lying in bed when I heard the phone ring. It was 7:30am. I was awake but I wasn't ready to get up yet. I could hear my mom's voice on the phone but I couldn't make out what she was saying.

A few minutes later, I heard a knock on my door.

---

[6]John Hopkins Medicine. "Osteogenesis Imperfecta." The John Hopkins University. 2023. hopkinsmedicine.org/health/conditions-and-diseases/osteogenesis-imperfecta#:~:text=Osteogenesis%20imperfecta%20(OI)%20is%20an,range%20from%20mild%20to%20severe.

"Lorna, get up and come out here. I have some sad news to tell you."

Huh?

I immediately felt a knot form in my stomach. I knew something was very wrong, but I couldn't imagine what it could be.

I came out of my room, still in my pjs, and sat down at the kitchen table to hear what my mother had to say.

"That was Karen on the phone. Last night, Carrie was helping her mom do the dishes after supper and she had a bad asthma attack. They called the ambulance to get her to the hospital but she didn't make it."

She didn't 'make it'?

I blinked a few times. I had to consciously sort through what that meant.

She didn't make it. Meaning, she died?

My friend and classmate. Fourteen years old. I had just been playing cards and eating pizza with her two days earlier.

Dead? She is fourteen! I just saw her!

We had all known for nine years that her asthma was severe, but we just thought that meant she couldn't push herself playing sports like the rest of us could.

Nut Bags and Num-Nums

This was why she died? Because her asthma was so bad it could take her life without warning?

She had been helping her mom with dishes.

Who dies while doing dishes?

I was so confused. And stunned. And sad.

She hadn't even been running around the house. She was doing dishes. And it had killed her.

I went back into my room and closed the door.

***

A few days later, I was in the balcony of the Lutheran church in Hanna attending the afternoon funeral service for my classmate and friend. It was December 24th. Christmas Eve. For me, it was Christmas. This was not the way things were supposed to be on Christmas. And I felt so sad for Carrie's parents.

My anger intensified when, during the service, four of my classmates who were sitting farther down the pew from me started messing around. They were giggling, chatting, not paying attention. Giggling! The older version of me would have leaned over to them and harshly whispered, "Shame on you. You didn't even like her. You were always mean to her. So why are you even here? And since you are here, behave yourselves and show some respect to her family and for those of us who *were* her friends." But I was fourteen and I was sitting on a church pew, sandwiched between my parents, listening to the pastor pay tribute to my friend.

I was also annoyed that my mother wouldn't take me out to the cemetery for the graveside service. The pastor had announced that all were welcome, but it was a cold day at -20C. And my mother had her own opinion about graveside services. In her mind, "Those are only for family," and she told me exactly that on that day.

So then why did Pastor announce that all are welcome?

My mother had the final word. We went home after the church service.

I spent the rest of that day locked in my room. I emerged when it came time for our Christmas Eve activities: dinner, church, touring around town looking at the Christmas lights, stopping at my grandparents' homes for hot chocolate and cookies, and then home to open gifts. It all seemed so meaningless that year—more like a duty or obligation. I was numb; I went through the motions but spent most of the rest of the Christmas break locked in my room.

A couple of days before the school year resumed, I guess my mom had decided that the mourning period was over. I had been in a slump ever since that early morning phone call.

"You need to get over this. Cheer up," she said. Something in her words put me off.

This was my mother, telling me, a fourteen-year-old kid, to "get over" the sudden, tragic death of one of my classmates.

Nut Bags and Num-Nums

Is there any getting over that? Ever? I asked myself. I'm sure she was just trying to prepare me for going back to school, but her comments felt cold and insensitive.

When I went back to school a few days later, I saw Carrie's empty desk in front of me in the next aisle. The mood in school, with both teachers and students, was more subdued than usual. No one talked about Carrie, but our teachers were softer and more forgiving of the rest of us for the next while, although nobody was pulling any antics either.

Forty years later, I still think of Carrie every Christmas Eve. Some years I light a candle for her in my living room and sit in the glow of it for a while. Part of me has always resented my mom saying what she did to me, as if grief, especially in a situation like that, is something that can be turned off at will, but I also suspect my mom was worried about me—that I would sink into a deep, lingering depression. She was, in her own way, trying to make sure I was going to be okay.

In 2022, both of Carrie's parents passed away within a few months of each other. I had seen them from time to time over the years when I returned to Hanna for the Shrove Tuesday pancake dinner at their church or at the grocery store. I never knew what to say to them. Even so many years later, whenever I saw them, the first thing to enter my mind was the image of Carrie. Part of me wanted to tell them that I still remember her, that I will always remember her as a fun and kind friend. But I guess a bigger part of me didn't want to remind them of that tragic Christmas. I didn't know if they would even remember me, and so I never talked to them. I only offered up a smile when our eyes met.

Gay

Jay was gay. (Erm, well, he still is). We were all certain of that early on in grade nine. But he never said a word to any of us throughout grade nine or high school about the topic. And my group of friends never brought it up except as a passing comment by some of us behind his back simply stating the fact. There was no judgement, no negativity, and no outward discrimination. It was simply an observation. To us, to label him or anyone else as gay was equivalent to saying, "Oh, she's the banker's daughter." No big deal. I was never witness to his receiving any bullying or discrimination.

Jay came out when he was twenty-five. I had just moved to Calgary after living in Japan for three years and was reconnecting with several of my high school classmates. I remember shortly after he came out, a group of us were together we said to each other, "Oh my GOD, it's about time! NOW can we finally talk about this with him?" For years, we only wanted to assure him that we had known all along and that we didn't care. We were his friends. Full stop. I was relieved and happy for him once he came out because I immediately saw an increase in his self-confidence and self-assuredness. I thought, *Finally, he can truly be who he is without worrying that we might judge or shun him.*

What I didn't know until reaching my fifties was that Jay was singled out by a few of our classmates that first year he entered our school.

"Yeah, your memory of what happened in those days is a little different than mine."

He laughed as he filled me in.

"Donald was constantly threatening to beat me up. Every day when I walked home from school, he was either in front of or behind me, always taunting me, telling me he was going to beat the crap out of me. And Andrew was just mean to me, calling me names all the time—fag, fairy, all that."

"I had no idea any of that was going on!"

"Yeah, I hated grade nine," he continued. "The whole first year we lived in Hanna, I wanted to go away to a private school somewhere else. Did you know I almost moved away to go to Bible school for grade ten?"

"WHAT? You? In Bible school?"

"Yeah. How's that for ironic? A gay kid going to Bible school to get away from being bullied."

But he stayed, and by halfway through grade ten, he had established his circle of friends, which overlapped with mine. He looks back on those days as a struggle and a time when he, like most teenagers, was searching for his identity.

"The 80s music had a huge impact. Culture Club, The Eurythmics. When we started to see people like Boy George and Annie Lennox on TV, suddenly someone like me didn't seem so different any more," he told me.

"But I also look back at it as a time that shaped me and my attitudes," he continued. "Now, I feel protective of the younger generation in the gay community and I feel like I can help them through their struggles of having people judge or discriminate against them."

Death is Toast

My friends and I reached the end of junior high in 1984, smack in the middle of the decade of big hair, neon clothes, and MTV. These details permeated our lives. We separated naturally into groups based on our musical preferences. I was big into Michael Jackson, and *Thriller* had just been released. A group of four of my classmates devoted themselves to Duran Duran, each girl picking one of the band members as their own and adopting the band members' names as their nicknames. Jay was a fan of Culture Club and the Eurhythmics.

We showed up for school wearing our parachute pants, headbands, leg warmers, dangly earrings, and off-the-shoulder tops. I had a pair of neon yellow pants and banana-shaped dangly earrings to match. The boys all started wearing polo shirts, and I switched from sneakers to boat shoes. We glued ourselves to MTV to catch all the latest music videos, and I practiced my moonwalk in my parents' basement. We didn't get MTV on the farm, but on one of the two channels we could get was a half-hour show once a week called *Video Hits*. Whenever I was at Karen's house in town, we watched MTV.

My friends and I alternated our musical purchases between LPs, 45s, and cassette tapes for those of us who had acquired Sony Walkmans. On our school ski trips to the Rockies, which took about five hours one way, someone was always in charge of bringing a cassette player and whoever had tapes would contribute them to the entertainment. Mr. Ghidina was wonderful about letting us blast AC/DC on the cassette player as long as we wanted to during those bus rides.

As we neared the end of our grade nine year, the guidance counsellor from the high school paid a visit to talk to us about our looming high school years.

"There are two streams you can choose from," he told us. "The matriculation stream is for those who plan to go to university, and the other stream is for those who don't."

Panic ensued. I felt like I had to plan my whole life with only a few weeks to think about it.

God forbid I choose the wrong stream!

Depending on which stream I took, certain doors would be open and others would not.

Despite being an 80 to 90 per cent student in all subjects in junior high, I was in a pressure situation at the end of grade nine. Self-doubt took over.

I'd better take the non-matriculation stream. I worry that I'm not smart enough for matric. What if I fail?

But what if I don't take the matriculation stream and find that the other stream is too easy? Then it's too late! And if I take the non-matriculation stream, I won't be able to go to university!

I felt like at the age of fourteen, I had to make one decision that would determine the rest of my life.

Nut Bags and Num-Nums

The argument with myself continued in my brain for several days until rational thought and my mother's pushing won the tug-of-war. Of course I would take the matriculation stream, and of course I would do fine. I wasn't at the top of my class, but I was shadowing those who were. I was certainly capable of succeeding in high school. Millions of teenagers do, and if I wanted to go to university and pursue my dream of being a teacher, I had to go for it.

***

When I began senior high school, as was the case when I started junior high, some of my teachers had taught Janice and others were new. And as was the case with every other aspect of my life, my sister's coming before me created expectations and images of who I was or should be.

"Ah, another good one," Mr. Ryerson, our English teacher, said to me on the first day when he asked us, row by row, to introduce ourselves.

Eek. Yeah, there's pressure on me to do well in English class now, I thought to myself.

Janice had done well in his class. He expected the same of me. And his expectations never wavered.

Halfway through my grade ten year, I got back an essay that we had handed in. He hadn't graded mine. When he handed it to me, he looked at me and simply said, "You can do better."

He was right. And so I redid the essay, putting forth more effort than I had the first time. The expectations Mr. R.

(everyone called him that) placed on me encouraged me rather than making me feel incapable. He had a knack for making the kids in his class feel valued and worthy. With those four words and the kindness in his eyes when he said them, he left a lifelong inspiration within me to always aim to do my best.

A couple of months into my grade eleven year, Mr. R. told us about a poetry contest that the Royal Canadian Legion was running and he encouraged us to enter. He was looking at me when he made this announcement.

I procrastinated, as always, once again living up to one of my nicknames: Last-Minute Lorna. Finally, the night before the deadline, I convinced myself that I should enter the contest. My teacher was expecting me to, and as someone who was passionate about writing, I owed it to myself to come up with a poem to enter.

I sat at the kitchen table and scribbled out a few ideas. After working on it for a while (I always say I wrote this poem in ten minutes, but it was more like an hour or two that I worked on it), I was happy with it and signed off for the night.

The next day, I submitted my poem to my teacher and was delighted a couple weeks later to learn I had won first place in the local competition. My poem would go on to compete at the regional level.

More waiting. And more good news. My poem won first place at the regional level! It was going to be competing for provincial honours.

Nut Bags and Num-Nums

In the final stage of the competition, my poem came in second place. And the best part about this? There was prize money in the mix at each level. My poem earned me $110 total. In 1984, that was a hefty sum for a short piece of writing!

My prize-winning poem:

Reminding Us

>Sunlight bouncing off the helmet,
>Bronze glistening in the sun.
>Ten feet above me
>Is this man. A stranger to me.
>All I know is a name
>And a cause
>For this work of art
>Never seen by the name
>Yet bringing a tear
>To every eye gazing upon it.
>The message is clear
>Without reading the inscription.
>The gun, the uniform
>Displaying proudly
>This statue's reason for being.
>It is there to remind me
>Though reminding I need not.
>For how could one forget
>The bloody, gruesome sacrifice
>Given by this soldier
>And others not so easily named?
>It was they who gave their lives—
>The hope of building a dream,
>Shattered in the trenches.
>What pain and suffering!
>Endured only because
>Of determined commitment,
>Of pride, and of love

Nut Bags and Num-Nums

> For us, the promise of the future.
> For them, the statue of honour
> We will remember even after
> The statue, like he, has crumbled down.

I wrote a lot of poetry in my high school years. Most of it is crap, which I even recognized at the time, and most of it is also really depressing because I struggled with depression in high school, but I was proud of my Remembrance Day poem.

I'm a real writer! Complete strangers have read and liked my writing. AND I GOT PAID!

***

Mr. R. was everyone's favourite teacher. *Everyone.* Even now, decades after graduating from high school, I have never heard one former student of his say they didn't love and respect him.

He was a pencil of a man. His clothes hung off him, and he had a well-trimmed but ever-present beard and moustache. He wore square, black-rimmed glasses and stood about five foot eight or nine. He probably weighed about a hundred pounds. Maybe less. He was our answer to Willie Nelson; we all joked about how he was probably at Woodstock when he was younger. He never 'fessed up to that, but he did tell us some stories about hitchhiking in California when he was younger. He was as hippie as hippies come but he always wore a suit jacket and was well kept.

And he was smart. And damn funny.

To my knowledge, no one ever heard him laugh. The closest we ever came to hearing him laugh was seeing the sides of his mouth twitch a bit under his beard when he couldn't help but let the beginnings of a smirk eke out. Now and then we could see his shoulders shaking a bit, but he never laughed audibly.

And he was encouraging. Even when he was "insulting" his students, we all took it as how it was intended—a good ribbing.

He taught us a poem that had the word wench in it and he asked who in the class knew what the word meant. My friend Karen abruptly stuck up her hand and proudly announced, "My dad has a wench on his truck!"

"Karen, why did you leave your brain at home today?" he asked above all of our laughter.

Karen was one of his main scapegoats because English wasn't one of her favourite subjects and so she didn't put much effort in. Mr. Ryerson attended the Lutheran church and knew her from there, and she also babysat his kids, so he knew she was a good sport and would tolerate his teasing.

On another occasion, he picked her as one of those reading aloud for another piece of literature we were studying. The character he chose for her was the Harpy, but alas, Harpy had no actual words to say in the text. There were spots where Harpy entered the scene, but Karen was lost.

"What am I supposed to say? There aren't any words for me to read."

"Well, what is a harpy?"

"A fairy?" some guessed.

Nut Bags and Num-Nums

"Not bad. But not quite."

According to Merriam-Webster, a harpy is

1. a foul malign creature in Greek mythology that is part woman and part bird
2. a: a predatory person
3. b: a shrewish woman[7]

Once we were clear on what a harpy was, we knew darn well his first choice for this character was premeditated.

"So, what do you think a harpy sounds like when she speaks, Karen?" he asked.

The left side of Karen's mouth turned up slightly in her trademark smirk.

"Hm hm hm hm hm hm."

"Very good, Karen. Proceed," he nodded to the student who had the next line to read.

Our other classmates took their turns, reading their parts, and every time the script indicated "Harpy", we all looked at Karen who faithfully "read" her part.

"Hm hm hm hm hm hm hm hm hm hm hm hm hm."

Bla bla bla bla bla bla.

---

[7] Merriam-Webster.com Dictionary, s.v. "harpy," accessed April 15, 2023. merriam-webster.com/dictionary/harpy.

Bla bla bla bla bla bla.

Bla bla bla bla bla bla.

"Hm hm hm hm hm hm hm hm."

Bla bla bla bla bla bla.

Bla bla bla bla bla bla.

"Hm hm hm hm hm hm hm."

By the time my classmates finished the reading, several of us had sore jaws from laughing at our poor Harpy.

***

We were the first group of students to filter through our high school once computers were introduced to the world, but still, only a few of us started to type up our English essays on computer or typewriter. Mom had an electric typewriter at home, and because I was doing well in Typing class and enjoyed it, I typed my essays rather than writing them by hand. Some of the boys in my class had, shall we say, "unique" handwriting, and so one of them hired me to type his essays for him. I charged a dollar a page. I served him well until I made one innocent typo on one of his essays for Mr. R. When my classmate got his essay back, he showed me that our teacher had noticed I had typed on the title page "Brain" instead of "Brian" and commented in his read pen, "Doubtful."

***

Mr. R. introducing us to *The Canterbury Tales*, more modern classis such as *1984*, and of course Shakespeare. He had a knack for making the old stuff interesting.

One of the classic poems we studied was John Donne's *Death, Be Not Proud:*

Death, be not proud (Holy Sonnet 10)
John Donne – 1571-1631

>Death, be not proud, though some have called thee
>Mighty and dreadful, for thou are not so;
>For those whom thou think'st thou dost overthrow
>Die not, poor Death, nor yet canst thou kill me.
>From rest and sleep, which but thy pictures be,
>Much pleasure; then from thee much more must flow,
>And soonest our best men with thee do go,
>Rest of their bones, and soul's delivery.
>Thou art slave to fate, chance, kings, and desperate men,
>And dost with poison, war, and sickness dwell,
>And poppy or charms can make us sleep as well
>And better than thy stroke; why swell'st thou then?
>One short sleep past, we wake eternally,
>And death shall be no more; Death, thou shalt die. [8]

By the time we studied this poem, we knew we had to study a Shakespeare play every year of high school, and we also knew he was trying to endear us to the classics. Still, the language of this older stuff presented a challenge to teenagers who would

---

[8] Donne, John. "Death, be not proud (Holy Sonnet 10)." poets.org/poem/death-be-not-proud-holy-sonnet-10.

have rather been reading contemporary favourites such as, *Cujo, The Hunt for Red October,* or *Archie's Digest.*

"So, let's talk about this poem," he started. "What figures of speech do you see?"

"In the first line, the speaker is talking directly to death, so that's personification," Little Miss Brown-noser piped up.

"Very good, Lorna. What else?"

Ok whew. That part was easy. Now I'm off the hook. Other people can tackle the rest of this thing, hee hee.

I sat back, leaving my classmates to chime in on the harder parts of the poem.

"What is the narrator trying to say about death?"

The class discussion revolved around the points Donne makes about poison and war and sickness and how all of these events lead to death, but Mr. R. had a hard time getting any of us to see the main theme of the poem until he directed us to zero in on the last half of the last line: "Death, thou shalt die."

"Death is toast!" one of my classmates piped up.

"Thank you for sharing your genius with us, Allan."

The Cowfur Mobile

My high school classmates have been razzing me about this for decades, and I know they will continue to do so until the day I die. I'm 100 per cent sure someone will tell this story at my funeral, too.

Farm kids don't have the option to work at the convenience store a short walk or bus ride away from home like town or city kids do. Until I was old enough to drive, I couldn't get a job in town, so I had to find ways to make extra money from our parents or neighbours.

In my pre-teen years, my main sources of income were my weekly allowance, which was five dollars, and hunting gophers. Sometimes Janice and I offered to do extra chores for a bit of extra money.

Both Janice and I got our first real job from the man who owned a large chunk of land adjacent to ours. Clarence was an older gentleman, a long-time family friend, who ran yearlings on his land every summer. Every fall he sold them and the land was vacant during the winter. Clarence's main land and homestead were a couple hours' drive away, so he wasn't close enough to keep a constant eye on the cattle he ran near us during the summer. When my sister got old enough, he hired her to check on his cattle. He applied for and received a grant provided by the Alberta government at the time for summer student employment; the grant covered most of her wages.

Nut Bags and Num-Nums

The job description was simple: Ride down to his land on her horse, count the cattle to make sure none were missing, check on them to see if any were sick, and report to him if anything was awry. She was to check on them two or three times a week, and it took a couple of hours each time.

When Janice moved away from home, I took over this job.

I was terrible at it. I've only ever had two jobs that I was really bad at: this one and working as a server at a restaurant, and for similar reasons. I have a bad short-term memory, and I'm not good at keeping track of too many things at once. The tricky part about counting the cattle was trying to keep track of which ones I had counted and which ones I hadn't while they were moving around. Often, I had to start over or herd them in a different direction so the ones I hadn't counted yet didn't mix with the ones I had counted.

Any time an animal looked sick or was in distress, I told my dad, who then either looked into it himself or reported my findings to Clarence.

I held this job in high school even after I had obtained my driver's license.

The three-mile road between our house and the highway was a dirt road and sometimes the gravel was quite loose, especially if it had just been graded. A Texas gate (cattle crossing) separated Clarence's land from ours on the road and a regular barbed-wire fence separated his pastureland from ours.

I was rushing back to school for a practice of the drama club's production of *Bye Bye Birdie*. I left home knowing I was running late, so I put my foot on the pedal a little harder than usual to try and make up some time.

Over the first half mile, I increased my speed, gaining confidence that I was going to make up some time before hitting the highway and risking a speeding ticket. Near the end of that first mile, though, I hit a loose patch of gravel and the car started fishtailing. I was rapidly nearing the Texas gate and to my horror, I saw about eight of Clarence's animals standing on the road on the other side of the gate, chewing their cuds and staring at the sage green Plymouth land yacht I was driving.

Oh shit. Shit shit SHIT SHITSHIT! I'm gonna hit the fencepost on one side of the Texas gate!

But I cleared the gate and then ...

Cattle are stupid. When a car approaches, they don't move. They stand there and stare at it.

BLAM! I slammed into one of the steers. The animal bounced onto the hood of the car. I was horrified, thinking I had killed it.

Nope. The beast rolled off the hood and hobbled away, clearly hurting in one of its legs. The others finally clued in that this wasn't a normal situation and they scuttled away.

I had no time to be in shock. I took a deep breath, made sure I had indeed not killed any animals, and took off again.

When I got to the school, I phoned my mom.

"Hi. I'm at the school but I had an accident on the way."

Nut Bags and Num-Nums

"What happened?"

"I lost control on the gravel and hit one of Clarence's steers. The steer is okay, and the car is dented on the front a bit but I can still drive it, and I'm okay."

"We'll deal with this when you get home."

The only real damage to the car was to the hood, which was crumpled a bit. Mom and Dad checked the car when I got home and gave me a good scolding about driving too fast. The whole event blew over fairly quickly.

Except ... in my worry about getting into trouble with my parents about the car, I forgot about Clarence, who came over to check on his cattle himself a few days later. He asked my dad if he knew anything about one of his animals being lame.

Shit!

The animal had no permanent injuries. But I felt like I was a bad employee not only because I could never keep track of how many damn animals were in the pasture every time I checked them, but now I had tried to commit vehicular cow-o-cide on one of them and hadn't even informed Clarence that I had injured his animal.

The car was essentially mine at that point because my mom had bought a new car, so I drove it to school a lot and to town to meet friends. My parents didn't get the damage fixed, probably because the horrendous teasing I endured from that point on served as greater punishment than anything my parents could do to me. For the rest of my high school days, my friends referred to it as Lorna's Cowfur Mobile because it had tufts of the steer's hair stuck in the cracks and creases in the hood. The hood also had to be held down with a bungie cord.

Our high school yearbook that year had a "Do You Remember ..." section, and so I'm forever memorialized in the yearbook:

Do you remember ... the time Lorna tried to make ground beef with her car?

We Felt Seen

Grade twelve. The end of high school was looming, which meant that many of us would be moving away, and most of us from the only home we'd ever known and from people we had known all our lives.

Because I had my sights set on being a teacher from the time I was eight, my plan was to go to university, get my teaching degree, and then teach high school English. Ideally, I wanted to teach in another country, but when I was in high school, I convinced myself that that was out of the realm of possibility. It would be jarring enough to go away to university. And then who knows where I would land. One step at a time though. I started applying to post secondary schools.

My guidance counsellors were telling me that the University of Lethbridge was considered the best program for training teachers. If I wanted a job after university, employers would look more highly on a degree from Lethbridge than from the other two universities in Alberta at that time: Calgary and Edmonton. I had no desire to move to Edmonton. I had been to the city probably all of three times. Even though it was only thirty minutes farther than Calgary (and actually, the same distance as Lethbridge), it was a big city that I wasn't accustomed to and therefore, I didn't consider the University of Alberta.

I quickly crossed Calgary off my list, as well. The city was just too big. With the University of Lethbridge having the reputation it did, and with the population of Lethbridge being only 60,000 people instead of several hundred thousand like Calgary, moving to Lethbridge would be a big enough change for a timid, self-conscious, weird rural kid. I applied to Lethbridge, but I also applied to Camrose Lutheran College, where I could do my first two years of university and then transfer to either Calgary, Lethbridge, or Edmonton for my last two years.

I got accepted to both places.

The wrinkle was that Camrose Lutheran College was also offering me a $500 music scholarship. That was enough money to pay for one semester of tuition! With my parents' money tied up in the farm, that five hundred bucks provided a strong temptation. But I ultimately turned it down.

I liked the idea of going to Camrose, but I didn't like the idea of having to move to a new city again after two years. I decided to head straight to Lethbridge and do my whole four-year program there.

But my classmates were headed elsewhere. Many of them were going to Calgary, either to attend the University of Calgary or The Southern Alberta Institute of Technology (SAIT). Others were staying in Hanna to work or help their parents on the farm with the goal of ultimately taking over the farm. Only two of us were headed to Lethbridge: me and my friend Kelly.

Kelly and I were good friends, but I knew I would otherwise be surrounded by strangers. I have never been comfortable in crowds where I know no one and have to make small talk. If I make new friends, it's usually because someone approaches and befriends me. I was terrified of all the unknown looming.

Nut Bags and Num-Nums

And I was failing Chemistry by the mid-term of the first semester in grade twelve. I had never failed a course before. I was used to being an honour student, and to have a 48 per cent on my report card was the ultimate shame. I dropped the class after those mid-term report cards came out, grateful that we only needed one grade twelve level Science course in order to graduate. I was doing well in Biology.

Around the halfway point of my grade twelve year, my mom had an operation. Nothing life-threatening, but she was in the hospital for several days. Until I was in grade ten, my mom had been home almost every day when I came home from school. The only exceptions were if she was in town picking up groceries or running other errands or out on our property somewhere helping my dad. When I reached grade ten, my mom went back to work full-time and so I came home to an empty house each day. I was fourteen, but I felt like a young child who had been abandoned. I had always been close to my mom and I had always taken for granted that she would be home. Coming home to an empty house was a big adjustment until I started to take advantage of that time alone to talk on the phone with my friends, go for a ride on my horse, or raid the freezer for cookies or Nanaimo bars to snack on while reading whatever book I was obsessed with at the moment.

But when she had her operation, for some reason, that feeling of abandonment returned. She was in the hospital for five days, and on the third day, Dad took me to the hospital to visit her. I sat on the chair in her room silent, sullen, and staring at the floor.

"Is she like this at home, too?" my mom asked my dad.

"Yuh." My dad mumbled his reply.

Too much was changing in my life all at once. My friends were turning eighteen and drinking in the bar, everyone was making plans for moving away from home, including me, and now my mom was in the hospital. I knew her situation wasn't serious, but I felt threatened. My comfortable life was on the verge of being taken away from me.

When she asked my dad that, I recognized that I was depressed, but I didn't understand why. I had a good life, and moving away from home to go to university was a, positive step forward into the next phase of my life. But I was struggling.

And so I did something that had become a habit at that point. I wrote a poem:

Thawing the Frost

>You chose the road least travelled,
>But how could you have known?
>I stand at this diversion
>Just waiting to be shown.
>
>Which is the path best for me?
>How did you make your choice?
>Was there a hand to lead you?
>Was there a guiding voice?
>
>I stand here where you pondered
>The path that you should take.
>I face that same decision.
>Confused. Alone to make.

Nut Bags and Num-Nums

Alone to thaw the frosted
Secrets that each path holds.
The frost hides all the flowers,
Clues hidden by the cold.

I cannot thaw the frosty
Veil that hides details
Of what lay in store for me
Along each of these trails.

I must choose with great caution,
Closely examining
Each path and consequences
These roads of life will bring.

(February 13, 1987)

And then I started hurting myself.

Suicide. That's what depressed people resort to, and I'm pretty sure I'm depressed. So I should consider suicide.

I brainstormed all the ways I knew people took their lives.

Poison.

Not a chance. I can barely choke down a piece of liver. There's no way I'd be able to down enough bleach or gasoline to poison myself. I love the smell of gasoline, but I'm pretty sure it doesn't taste good. I'd give up after the first sip.

Pills.

Nut Bags and Num-Nums

Nothing in the house is strong enough. I'd have to take a gallon or two of Tylenol, and no one in this house is on any prescription pills! What would I use?

Gun.

Dad only owns a .22 rifle. My arms aren't long enough to point it at my head and pull the trigger. Plus, I'd probably miss completely and shoot a hole in the damn wall instead of my head. Then I'd get in the worst trouble of my life and I'd never be allowed near the gun again.

Knife.

There's NO WAY I could stab myself. Sure, I can help Dad with treating or butchering the animals—no problem—but for God's sakes, I fainted last time I was at the hospital and they took blood for a blood test. The moment the tip of the knife blade touched my skin, I'd propel the knife across the room and run screaming from myself.

How the heck did Romeo and Juliet go through with this?

So, I scratched my face. I had slightly longer fingernails on my right hand, good for guitar picking. I stood in front of the mirror in the bathroom at home one evening and scratched at my right cheek until it turned red and raw and burned. My cheek hurt too much for me to continue to the point it would bleed, but I had a noticeable, flaming-red scrape on my cheek, about an inch long.

I went to school the next day desperately waiting for someone to say something about my cheek so that I could tell someone that I was struggling—so that I could find support. No one said a word.

All that pain for nothing, I thought. *No one cares.*

I knew that wasn't true, but the non-response from my classmates was a bit of a revelation.

There's no point in hurting myself. It isn't getting me what I need.

Even though no one said a word to me about my cheek, our assistant principal pulled me aside one day after class for a chat a few weeks later.

"What's your plan for after graduation?" he asked me.

"I was going to go to university in Lethbridge for my teaching degree, but I think I'll stay home and work for a year instead."

"Why do you want to take a year off?"

"So I can make money."

"Did you apply for a student loan?"

"Yeah, I should be able to get enough money for the year, but I want to save up more of my own money first."

I didn't have a plan. I was just getting cold feet about moving away from home, and he sensed as much what with my gloomy mood for the past several weeks.

He launched into a private math lesson for me, showing me on a piece of paper how teachers' salaries work. You start at the bottom and work your way up. Each year of experience gets you a bit of a raise until you have X number of years' experience. Then, you reach the top of the pay grid and you stay there.

Nut Bags and Num-Nums

"If you take a year off now and work, you'll make minimum wage or slightly higher. But if you go to university right away, you'll graduate four years from now instead of five. You'll be at the top of the pay grade eleven years after that. By taking a year off before going to university, you're robbing yourself of one year of making the highest salary. You'll shortchange yourself financially at the end of your career."

This was the brilliant Math teacher whose classes were over my head, but two things resonated with me during that conversation. One was that his math for this scenario made sense. The other ... he had noticed I was in a mental pit. He saw a student who was struggling and he went out of his way to speak to me one on one, to coach me out of my despair.

I walked away from that conversation feeling seen, feeling heard, feeling like an intelligent, respectable man had my best interests at heart and had taken the time and made the effort to encourage me to lift my chin up and pursue what had been my only life goal for ten years. He was exactly the type of teacher I wanted to become.

***

I can't begin to understand what it would feel like to be the only gay kid in a rural high school in the 1980s. I'm sure on some level my friend Jay felt very alone; even though he had a strong circle of friends, there was a big part of his identity that none of the rest of us could relate to and in fact no one ever acknowledged. Since he didn't talk about his sexuality in high school, we certainly didn't bring it up with him.

Nut Bags and Num-Nums

But remember, Mr. Ryerson introduced us to *The Canterbury Tales* ... and one of them, "The Miller's Tale", is a memory that sticks with Jay to this day. Here's a section of it:

> Up rose this jolly lover Abaslon
> In gayest clothes, garnished with that and this;
> But first he chewed a grain of licquorice
> To charm his breath before he combed his hair.
>
> ....
>
> And at the window out she put her hole,
> And Absalon, so fortune framed the farce,
> Put up his mouth and kissed her naked arse
> Most savourously before he know of this.
> And back he started. Something was amiss;
> He knew quite well a woman has no beard,
> Yet something rough and hairy had appeared.
> 'What have I done?' he said. 'Can that be you?'
> 'Teehee!' she cried and clapped the window to.[9]

Of course we thought it was delightfully scandalous that our English teacher was introducing us to dirty poems and other literature that talked about sex, and in this case, pubic hair.

"Ew, he kissed her 'down there'!" one of our classmates exclaimed.

Mr. Ryerson looked Jay in the eye.

---

[9] Chaucer, Geoffrey. "The Miller's Tale." *The Canterbury Tales: An Illustrated Selection Rendered Into Modern English by Nevill Coghill.* (1977). 119-122. Middlesex: Penguin Books. P. 199-122.

"You'll never have to worry about that," he told this young man, his trademark smirk starting to show beneath his beard.

Jay still remembers that moment and says of Mr. R., "You know, he was the kind of teacher who met every kid where they were at, and he knew exactly how to pull each of us in. As a kid coming to terms with being gay, when he said that bit about kissing her 'looter' and how I would never have to worry about kissing a woman's 'beard,' I felt seen. When he looked at me and said that, of course it was funny, but it was also like he was telling me it's ok to be who I am."

***

Whenever I look back at that period of my grade twelve year, I recognize that this was when I first became aware that I have depression and anxiety. I always have, and I know that I always will. I can now pinpoint times earlier in my childhood when symptoms of depression were evident. I struggled with controlling my emotions as a kid until I realized that throwing a temper tantrum did not achieve my desired result. My parents didn't give in and grant me what I was demanding; they ignored me unless my tantrums persisted. In those cases, I got scolded or spanked. As I neared my teens, I realized that all I was accomplishing by pouting and throwing a tantrum was looking like a spoiled brat, and I started to try and manage my emotions.

I see my temper tantrums, my other outbursts, my internalization of my frustrations were all symptoms of a struggle I've always had: worrying that what I was doing was wrong, worrying that I wasn't good enough, and battling with what I call "the monster living inside me" who still controls my rational thoughts now and then. I was, and still am at times, terrified of what might happen if I make a mistake or do something that someone else deems as "wrong".

"Don't raise your hand during the cattle auction," Mom used to warn me. "If you raise your hand, that means you're bidding on the cattle. You might end up buying a cow!"

"Lorna, sit on your hands," the monster told me as I sat between my parents at the auction mart. "Yes, your nose is itchy, but if you even MOVE your hand, you will end up buying a cow, and how are you going to pay for a cow?"

OH NO! I don't want to accidently buy a cow! If I buy a cow, my parents will have to pay for it. They can't afford it. I'll be the reason my family goes broke! And then my parents and sister will hate me forever!

I endured countless itchy and runny noses at auctions for fear of taking my hands out from under my legs.

I wasn't so much afraid of the typical things like spiders, snakes, or injury. And even in my teenage years I didn't stress out about being liked. What hobbled me was the fear of doing anything wrong. To me, getting judged, laughed at, scolded, or corrected was the worst punishment anyone could inflict on me. I would have rather had a spanking. But more than anything, being told or even telling myself I was wrong about anything made me feel inadequate, inferior, less than.

"LOOOORRRNA," the monster called out to me a few years ago, "don't quit your teaching job. You're walking away from a salary of almost $100,000 a year, good benefits, summers off, and guaranteed employment until you are ready to retire. Why would you *choose* to walk away from all of that?"

"Because I *know* I need to make a change. Every time I have left a job, the next job I have moved to was better than the previous one. I've always made good decisions when it comes to that part of my life."

"What if this the one time that's different?" the monster argued. "You're moving toward *nothing*. You're thinking of starting your own business, which you have no experience in. What if you don't make any money for years? Or ever? You will end up destitute, homeless, friendless, purposeless."

"I know. It's a huge risk. Let's see—how long can I sustain myself on no income?"

"Probably about six months. Then your life will be in ruins."

It took a lot of hard work in my adult years until I finally started to break through the handcuffs my constant worry has always had me in. A turning point was chewing on some good advice from a psychologist who pointed out to me that instead of focusing on "What if [insert worst case scenario] happens?" how about I change my perspective and focus on "What if [insert best case scenario] happens?"

Curfew

The best thing about having an older sibling is being able to watch and learn. Remember that TV show "What Not to Wear"? An older sibling naturally becomes a great in-house reality show of "What Not to Do", especially as a teenager.

My only sibling is almost four-and-a-half years older than I am. Close enough that we played together a fair bit as kids but a big enough spread that she went through the various stages of childhood almost fully before I entered that stage. She was in her final years of elementary school by the time I was in grade one. She was in high school by the time I started junior high, and she had already graduated and moved away before I finished junior high. When I was really little, I often puttered along, following her around, trying to mimic her; what kid doesn't want to be just like the older sibling they look up to?

As we got older she started to have the typical teenage-themed fights with Mom.

"Why can't I? All my friends are."

"If all your friends jumped off a bridge, would you want to do that, too?"

I observed and started to take mental notes on what prompted those fights.

Nut Bags and Num-Nums

"Your curfew is 11:30. It's past midnight. Where were you, and why are you late?"

"It's barely a minute after midnight. I'm not that late. And 11:30 is a stupid curfew. All my friends get to stay out way later than that."

"Where WERE you?"

"Out."

"Out where? Were you drinking?"

I'm not sure if I speak for all younger siblings but what's certainly true for me is that I wasn't necessarily a *better* kid than my older sister. I just had a chance to learn what not to do. I was better at being sneaky than she was.

She got in trouble for being out past curfew, but she came home more than half an hour after curfew. I wonder if I will be in trouble if I'm only five or ten minutes past curfew?

"Why didn't you call if you were going to be late?"

Ah, so the issue is that Mom didn't know she was going to be late. So, if I call and let her know that I'm going to be late, maybe I won't get yelled at.

One of the many differences between me and Janice is that she was never one to shy away from confrontation whereas I tended to clamp my mouth shut and walk away any time I was pulled into an argument or chastised for something, even if the other person was completely wrong or out of line. It wasn't until I was in my early 40s after my mom, from her death bed, told me, "You need to stand up for yourself more," that I started to do so.

Conflict of any kind gives me great anxiety, so I dreaded being witness to the fights my mom and sister got into, and I *definitely* didn't want to have the same types of arguments with my mom. I developed a strategy. Because, you know, *teenagers are so much smarter than their parents.*

My curfew, like my sister's, was 11:30, which I thought was ridiculously early, especially since it was a ten-minute drive from town back to our farm. That meant I had to leave whatever my friends and I were doing by 11:20 in order to make curfew. Most of my friends had later curfews, and many of them lived in town, so they could continue doing whatever we were doing until much later than I could. I resented my limits.

Most of the time, we weren't doing much. We weren't causing trouble, but we weren't doing anything productive or meaningful either. There wasn't much for teenagers *to* do at the time. Yeah, Hanna had a stripper bar, but nothing for teenagers.

There was one movie theatre in town. The whole time I was growing up, I was told that the building the theatre was in had been condemned long before I was even born. (I'm not sure if this was even true—likely not, but it was a great rumour.) It wasn't until after I left home that the theatre closed down, so we did have movies to go to once in a while. The theatre showed the same movie for at least two or three weeks. And the movies we got had been released and shown in the city movie theatres months prior. It was something to do but only once every three weeks or so unless you wanted to watch the same movie multiple times.

Nut Bags and Num-Nums

VCRs were starting to enter family homes. My parents bought a Beta machine, which quickly became obsolete, and then got a VHS machine. There was a video rental shop in town, so renting movies was always a good option.

By the time I got to high school, the bowling alley had shut down. Even when it was still open, the lanes were so warped that it didn't matter where you aimed the ball and how good you were at bowling. Your score was ultimately a matter of luck and whichever way the ball decided to turn depending on how much spin and weight you put on it.

We spent the majority of our Friday evenings driving main. Those of us who had vehicles or who were allowed to use our parents' vehicles piled as many friends as possible inside and drove back and forth, up and down Main Street all night. The town was about a mile from one end to another. At one end was a Red Rooster convenience store, and at the other was the Canada Grey Motor Inn, or The Goose, as we called it. Both had parking lots that served as great turnaround spots so that when we reached the end of Main Street, we could easily turn around and drive back the other way. Back and forth. For hours.

Everyone knew one another's vehicles, and so as we passed each other, we would wave, honk, and sometimes stop in the middle of the street and chat through the open windows. There were usually a lot of snacks involved, including slushies from the Red Rooster, and the 80s music was blaring. The worst infraction during these nights was the time one of my classmates, while driving past another friend, lifted up her shirt to flash the other person. Other than that, the smoking that some engaged in, and the complete waste of gas, our evenings driving main were innocent.

For the most part, our house parties were harmless, too. There was alcohol, but I don't recall anyone getting so drunk that they were in harm's way.

Not long after I had gotten my driver's license and was driving home from town one Friday night, I got a speeding ticket just as I was leaving town and nearing the highway. The RCMP officer pulled me over, asked for my license, and made me sit and squirm while he went back to his car to write me up a $20 ticket. I was mortified. To me, this was a horrible sin, and *I had done something wrong.* Would my parents take away my rights to drive their car alone?

When I got home I told my mom about the ticket. (I'm so honest I roll my eyes at myself sometimes: A few years ago, I posted a picture on Facebook of a parking sign in front of a dentist's office that said, "Parking for those who floss daily" with the message "I'm so honest, I parked *beside* this parking spot.") Mom didn't have much of a reaction other than a bit of a lecture. I had to pay the ticket out of my own money, of course. For the rest of high school, I tried to ease up on the gas pedal a bit. (It wasn't until I was in university that I got my next speeding ticket, and again, I was mortified. Since then, I've had "a few", including one incident a few years ago when I got camera tickets in the mail two days in a row. Ugh! They're a bit more than twenty bucks these days!)

Those of us who lived on farms had to drive home at the end of a Friday night of course. Even those who lived in town drove everywhere if they had a vehicle. That's just what we did.

Nut Bags and Num-Nums

We drove everywhere, even if it was easier to walk. One weekend when I was in my late thirties, I took a couple of friends from Calgary to Hanna for a day. We stopped at the bank to use the ATM and then got back into my vehicle. I drove one block to the restaurant and parked again.

One of my friends exclaimed, "We're here? This is as far as we're going?"

"Yes?"

I was puzzled as to why he was asking until my brain switched back to Calgary mode and I said, "Oh, this is Hanna! Nobody walks anywhere! We've always driven anywhere we're going, even if it's one block!"

So when there were house parties, there were lots of vehicles parked on the street, and since we all knew what everyone drove and where everyone lived, if someone didn't know about a party but drove past and saw the vehicles, they knew there was a party. These days, news of parties spreads on social media. Back then, it spread by driving around town and seeing whose vehicles were parked where.

If there was alcohol at house parties, most of us kept to a decent limit. I liked to think I was being responsible, and I almost always stopped after one or two drinks before I had to leave for my ridiculous curfew. I wanted to make sure I could safely drive home, and I wanted to make my curfew so that my mother wasn't waiting for me at the door, where she would smell my breath. I figured that if I were on time or, at worst, ten minutes late, she would stay in bed listening for the door. And if I was going to be five or ten minutes late, I usually tried to make sure I phoned her to let her know I was on my way so she would stay in bed and wait.

One night time got away from me, and so did the alcohol.

We were at Donald's house. It was a good-sized house party, and I had a few too many drinks. I wasn't falling-down drunk, but I really didn't want to drive after having four or five drinks. I wanted to give the alcohol time to get out of my system a bit more, so I phoned my mom just before 11:30, told her I would be leaving soon, and rejoined the party. I had stopped drinking at this point, but I knew I was in no shape to drive home, so I let a bit more time pass by. And then I completely lost track of time.

My car was parked in front of another friend's house, and it was unthinkable that I would walk from Donald's house to hers in the dark, even though Hanna was pretty much the safest place on the planet. Plus, I was having fun. Part of me was rebelling against my hated curfew, and part of me was trying to be responsible and wait to drive home until I had sobered up. By the time I went back to my friend's house with her, retrieved my car, drove home, and met my dad in the kitchen, it was 5:30am. Every light in the house was on, and my mom was not there. She had gone to town looking for me.

She knew all of my friends and where they lived, and she had seen my car parked in front of my friend's house. She knocked on the door and talked to my friend's mom, who told her that yes, the two girls were out together but she didn't know where. My friend didn't have a curfew, and her single mom wasn't concerned about where her daughter was.

Nut Bags and Num-Nums

When she got home about fifteen minutes after I did, I found myself in one of those types of discussions she had had with my sister, except I was not arguing. I was crying and apologizing for having worried her to the point that she had gotten the RCMP involved and was out looking for me around town with them. I didn't have the nerve to admit that I had been drinking and that I was trying to be responsible by not driving until several hours after I had last consumed alcohol. I figured that would just make the situation worse.

It was the only time my dad was ever up waiting for me on a Friday night, and it was the last time I broke curfew. It was also the only time in my life I was uncomfortable with the silence between me and my dad.

My quiet, unassuming dad got pulled into my antics again toward the end of my grade twelve year. Two of my classmates were getting married. There was a stag party for the boy at a community hall in the country on the opposite side of Hanna, half an hour's drive from my farm. Even though we knew it was a stag party, a group of my female friends and I decided to crash it because, after all, we'd all grown up together. Why not?

We entered the community hall to a round of cheers from all the boys.

"The peelers are here!"

We laughed and joined in the party for a while. This time, I made sure I left in time to get home in time for my curfew, and I only had two drinks. But my car had other ideas.

Nut Bags and Num-Nums

The radiator overheated. So, about ten minutes from the hall, I had to pull over, stop, and sit and wait either until the radiator cooled down or someone rescued me. It was long before the days of cell phones, so I had no choice but to sit alone in the dark on the side of a gravel road in a car whose hood was steaming, and wait. I was in the middle of the country, and there were no farms within walking distance.

Fortunately, two boys from my class drove by a few minutes later. They saw The Cowfur Mobile on the side of the road, pulled over, and realized the predicament I was in. They knew there was no driving my car for a few hours, so they took me home. Of course I was late for my curfew and hadn't called because we had no access to a phone, so my mom was up waiting for me. I had only had a couple of drinks and wasn't unfit to drive. Still, my mother wasn't impressed when I arrived home with alcohol on my breath, accompanied by two boys, telling her that the car was on the side of the road twenty miles away. She thanked the boys for bringing me home and we all went to bed. She didn't tear a strip off me, so I thought that was the end.

I should have known better.

At 6:00 the following morning. Mom started banging on my door. I had been looking forward to sleeping until about 9:00. Nope. My punishment this time was Mom dragging me out of bed nice and early.

"Get up! Your dad is going to take you to get the car."

It *had* to be at 6:00am. Because I had misbehaved. (And because she thought I was hungover. I wasn't, and so I did gain a bit of satisfaction in knowing that she wasn't torturing me as much as she thought she was.)

I dragged myself out of bed and my dad and I quietly drove to get the car, which was still sitting where I had left it. By then, the radiator had cooled down and I drove it while Dad followed to make sure I got home.

I went back to bed unchallenged.

The one time I was released from my curfew was the weekend of our graduation.

Grad weekend in Hanna has always been the May long weekend. On the Friday, the grade twelves were excused from classes to schedule in pictures and spend the day getting ready for the evening's ceremony. Each graduand was allowed to invite ten people, and I had meticulously made my list of aunts, uncles, grandparents, and a few close family friends. I had invited Lee, my guitar teacher, but he was living up in Northern Alberta and couldn't make it. The rest of my invitees were all there.

During the ceremony, one of my classmates and I were scheduled to give a tribute to our teachers. We had decided ahead of time who would say what, and he assured me he was ready. When we walked up on stage together, he started patting his pockets, pretending that he had lost his speech. I was ready to kick him, but it was all an act. He finally pulled his speech out, and we gave our tribute to those who had steered us through our three years of high school.

Nut Bags and Num-Nums

After the ceremony was a dance, and I stayed for a short while but as was typical, pretty much all the grads left soon after the dance started. Most went to the party.

Each year, someone offered to let the graduating class use part of their farmland for a grad party out of town. The party lasted the whole weekend. Some people camped out; others came and went. The party started Friday night, and the last attendees straggled home sometime on the Sunday. I skipped the Friday night party and went home shortly after the dance started to be with my parents and my invited guests. All my relatives were at my parents' house, and I spent the evening opening cards and gifts and visiting with these people who had been a significant part of my first eighteen years. Some of them asked me if I was going to the grad party.

"No. I'd rather be here with you," was my reply.

I could see my friends any day of the school year. Aunts and uncles had driven two hours or more one way to come to honour me at my high school graduation, so I wanted to spend the evening with my family. And I had plans to spend time with my friends over the rest of the weekend, anyway.

We had snacks, drinks, and lots of laughs. My mom and dad's side of the family knew each other; many of my aunts and uncles on both sides had lived in Hanna as children and/or teenagers even if they lived far away now, so it was a great time of reunion and enjoying each other's company.

I could have left home late that night after everyone left, but I knew if I did, I'd be showing up late to a party where everyone had been drinking for a while. Plus, there would be tons of people there I didn't know or didn't know well, and I also didn't want my family to think I was waiting for them to leave so I could join another party. I took a pass on the official grad party and enjoyed the time with my extended family.

On the Saturday night, however, I arranged to connect with some of my friends and head to the party site. The party started all over again, and a lot fewer people were there—fewer strangers and older people. Most people had gone for the Friday party, so the Saturday version was smaller and limited more to the actual graduating class and a few others who my classmates were close to. On this one, special occasion, I had permission from my mom to stay out all night and come home anytime on the Sunday, as long as I was intact.

I stayed out all night with my buddies enjoying what would be one of our last chances to do something like this before many of us left home to go to university. We knew that in the next six weeks, what remained of the school year, we would be busy with final exams and then many of us would be working over the summer. Come August, those of us who were setting off to university would be leaving, looking for a place to live in Calgary, Edmonton, or Lethbridge. Our time together was running short. We talked that night about our futures, how we would always be friends and would stay in touch even though some of us were heading to different cities. Some were staying in Hanna, and those of us who were leaving promised we'd be back often. We were young idealistic teenagers looking at the corners we were about to round.

Rapscallions

My classmates and I weren't bad kids. We were mischievous, but nobody got in trouble with the police (unless you count speeding tickets). We were typical teenagers who liked to nudge the limits.

Miniskirts made a comeback when I was in high school. Our school had a rule that no one could wear shorts to school, boys or girls, but miniskirts were allowed. The boys thought this was unfair since most boys wanted to wear shorts that were several inches longer than miniskirts, but they knew that if they dared, they would be told to change. Our student union president and vice president decided one day that as the representatives of our student population, they needed to protest and make their point.

They showed up at school in miniskirts.

Our principal saw them shortly after they entered the school that morning.

"Both of you, to my office, please."

They followed him.

When they came out of the office, several of us were waiting in the hallway to hear what had happened.

"He told us to go home and change," Allan said.

Nut Bags and Num-Nums

"That's it? Did you tell him why you wore miniskirts today?" one of my classmates asked.

"Yeah. We told him we are protesting that girls are allowed to wear miniskirts but boys aren't allowed to wear shorts because the miniskirts are shorter than our shorts. So if miniskirts are allowed, then we are gonna wear miniskirts. He told us that's not how it works and we needed to change into pants."

"That's not fair," a few of us chimed in.

"Yeah, I know, but he's not going to change his mind."

They had both brought a change of clothes, having anticipated this result. They got their pants out of their lockers and headed into the bathroom to change. Not before Captain Kodak got a great shot of them in their miniskirts for the school yearbook, though.

My peers dubbed me Captain Kodak in grade ten because I joined the yearbook committee and became the official yearbook photographer. I carried my camera with me everywhere, every day of the school year. My peers quickly learned to avoid me or to at least position themselves, when they saw me coming, in ways that would prevent me from getting a good picture of them. I had to become increasingly sneaky to catch them unaware and get good candid photos. Fortunately, there were also plenty of opportunities when both students and teachers were willing to pose for great photos.

One such instance was during Rodeo Week.

We had wild cow-milking competitions. Rubber gloves were stapled or otherwise secured to the balance beam from gym class, and they were then filled with water, which had a bit of milk added to it to make it look milky. Students formed a relay team. The first team member ran to the balance beam, "milked" the glove, which had holes poked in the fingers, to get a certain amount of milk, and then ran back to tag off to the next team member.

Barrel racing was pretty straightforward. Three pylons were set up in the gym in the pattern of a real barrel race. Racers mounted a tricycle and ran the same pattern as barrel races run in a rodeo arena.

We had a beer chugging contest using root beer instead of the real thing. This was also a relay. Two-litre bottles of root beer were emptied into *massive* paper cups, and each team member had to chug the (root) beer before the next team member could begin. There was a lot of belching after that event.

Bull riding is most people's favourite event at a rodeo, and it was no different for our Rodeo Week. We had an advantage in our town. Canadian bareback riding champion David Shields lived nearby and owned a mechanical bull. For one day each year, he donated the use of it to our high school, setting it up outside the school surrounded by several gym mats so that anyone who fell off, (which was nearly everyone at some point) was sure to have a safe, soft landing. David operated the bull for us. I remember riding on it, being somewhat scared but quickly realizing that he controlled the speed and rotation of the bull. He adjusted the speed and force depending on the skill of the rider, so no one was ever in for more than they could handle.

Nut Bags and Num-Nums

He made sure we all had a great, thrilling experience without getting hurt. I was impressed when our assistant principal got on the bull in his white dress shirt, tie, and dress pants to give it a go. And David himself always demonstrated how a pro gets the job done.

The most dangerous event, as it is in real life (other than the bull riding), was the chuckwagon races. The chuckwagon course was also marked with pylons in the gym, and two teams ran against each other for the fastest time. The chuckwagons were made of old toboggans. To the front of them was attached a hockey stick with bike bars extending from the end. Two "horses" (team members) pulled the wagon, which had one rider on it. There were always some spectacular crashes against walls or other racers.

The winners in each event earned points that counted toward a prize at the end of Rodeo Week for the team with the most points overall. The highlight of my Rodeo Week in grade eleven was when my team won the air band contest. I was dressed as Willie Nelson with yarn braids, my Wranglers, an invisible guitar, and my Willie Nelson T-shirt and headband, which I had bought when I attended his concert in Calgary months prior. We performed "On the Road Again" and annihilated the competition, which included some of our male classmates performing the ever-so-popular country and western classic (not), "The Wonderful Thing About Tiggers."

***

The year I entered grade ten was the first year my high school had computers. There was one Apple IIE, which was the coveted prize; we got to play games on it when we were done our course tasks or did other work to earn such a reward. The rest of the time, we were on clunky old DOS computers, learning how to program in BASIC.

I was surprised that I was in my element in Computer Science class. I was good at and loved Math up to high school but in grade ten I started to struggle with it. I also had a hard time with Chemistry, and I never even attempted Physics. But for some reason, I was fascinated by and seemed to have a knack for computer programming.

Our Computer Science teacher was also our assistant principal, so he always started class with a mini lecture for ten or fifteen minutes, instructing us on what to do to create a certain type of program. Then, he gave us an assignment to do and left the room for the rest of the eighty-minute period. It didn't take us long to realize this was his pattern, and so when he left the room, we took to delegating one person to do the programming assignment for the day, who would then share it with us, while the rest of us played games.

Despite our plagiarism, the worst trouble I got into in Computer class was for another type of laziness. These were the days of the five-inch floppy disks that were literally floppy, unlike the smaller, hard-cased floppies of the early 90s. They were square with a hole in the middle and were easily damaged if bent or if something was placed on top of them.

I needed to share my floppy with a classmate who was on the other side of the room and instead of getting up, walking over, and handing it to my classmate like a decent human would, I frisbeed it across the room, missing my friend and hitting the

Nut Bags and Num-Nums

corner of the desk. The floppy was dented and rendered useless. My teacher claimed my floppy, stapled it to the bulletin board, and titled it "What Not to Do in Computer Class."

I also signed up for Accounting class in all three years of high school. Our teacher was always well-dressed in a suit jacket and had a geeky sense of humour. He sometimes gave us snap "quiz-i-poos" but always warned us of upcoming "testi-westies."

My Accounting class was after lunch, and one day, one of my classmates was absent, so it seemed. It was a bright, sunny spring day, and this classmate wasn't exactly dedicated to his studies, so for him to be skipping class wasn't out of the realm of possibility. However, twenty minutes into class, he entered the room, dripping wet as if he'd emerged from a bathtub.

"Mr. Collier! Mr. Collier! I'm so sorry I'm late! I was on my way back to school after lunch but a big rainstorm suddenly came up! The wind was so strong! I was riding my bike and the wind kept pushing me back so hard, it took me forever to get here! And the rain was so strong, you can see I'm drenched! I'm so sorry I'm late."

After class that day, another student, who was also late, told us that he had seen this kid outside the school dumping buckets of water on himself before he entered the school.

I loved the idea of Chemistry class in high school but it quickly became too difficult for me. It wasn't long before I started tuning out.

We dutifully performed our assigned experiments, and once we were done and as time permitted, we then dumped all the chemicals within reach into our beakers and flasks to see what it would take to make pretty colours and explosions.

My favourite moment in Chemistry class was when my friend Darcy and I conducted our own brief experiment. At the end of class one day, I had an empty pop can. Our teacher had no problem with us drinking pop during class, and my pop can was empty when the bell rang. The pop can had two holes on the top—a bigger one and a smaller one. Darcy and I discovered that the bigger hole was exactly the right size to fit on the end of the faucet in the sink at our table in the back of the room. I screwed the can onto the end of the faucet and just as it secured itself firmly on the end, Darcy cranked the tap to turn on the water. Water went shooting out the small hole, straight up to the ceiling in true geyser fashion, and we bolted out the door to our next class. Our teacher never said a word to us about our pop can experiment.

***

Darcy and I needed a stapler for a school project we were working on. We decided to go to the office and see if we could borrow one from the school administrator.

On our way to the office, we devised our plan—the typical "one of us will cause a distraction and the other will steal the stapler and run" plan.

I sidled up to the front desk and smiled at the administrator.

"So, how are you today?" I batted my eyes and grinned. She immediately knew something was up.

"I'm good, Lorna. How are you?" She grinned back.

"Good. Yeah, I was just coming to chat with you because I haven't talked to you for a while. Just wondering how your day was going."

And then I started shuffling sideways toward the garbage can. I pretended I was throwing something in it, and then peered into it.

"Oh, look at this? What is this in here?"

She didn't fall for it. She stayed behind the counter.

"What is it you see in there?" she asked.

I turned around, not sure where I should take the conversation from there. Her not falling for my ruse was a turn of events I had not anticipated.

"Oh, look over there!" I pointed to the wall to the side, as I turned my back to the garbage can.

She still wasn't buying it. I could see the corners of her mouth turning up, surely waiting to see what exactly I was up to.

"There, on the wall! Don't you see that? It's a huge spider!" I exclaimed as I backed up, feigning shock and terror.

I ended up backing up too far and too quickly. I went crashing butt first into the garbage bin and fell inside. There I was, butt inside the garbage bin, arms and legs sticking out the top. I was stuck. And of course I was laughing uncontrollably.

So was the administrator.

"Oh, now I see what you mean!" she said. "There IS something strange in the garbage can!"

She only made me laugh harder, and Darcy, who was supposed to be absconding with the stapler, was also laughing.

"Help me!" I cried out.

I could barely breathe, between being scrunched in the garbage can and laughing myself silly.

Darcy was laughing too hard to help me and so there I stayed for several minutes. A few teachers came and went from the staff room, glancing at us as they passed by, rolling their eyes and laughing as they continued on their way.

Finally, Darcy calmed down enough to grip my hands, pull me over so that the garbage can tipped onto its side, and help me get out.

After I sheepishly returned the garbage can to its upright position and tucked it into the corner, the administrator asked us, "Why are you girls really here, anyway?"

"We need to borrow a stapler," Darcy and I said in unison.

She picked up the stapler, put it on the counter in front of us, and went back to sit at her desk.

***

Nut Bags and Num-Nums

I rarely got in trouble in school other than for the desk-cleaning incident in grade one, my fictional account of Bach's life and dramatic death, and yawning in grade seven Language Arts class. Our Chemistry teacher never mentioned the geyser Darcy and I created with the pop can. And when my teacher stapled my floppy disk to the bulletin board, he laughed and told me I had only disadvantaged myself because everything on the disk was now lost forever. I've always found it ironic that most of the incidents I got disciplined for in school were unintentional. When I was purposely being bratty, my teachers often looked the other way.

Looking through my own teacher's lens during and after sixteen years of working with high school kids, I suspect it was because my teachers knew I was a decent kid just being silly. The antics my friends and I got into were pretty harmless compared to beating people up, stealing, setting fires, or doing drugs. We were goofy kids who had no bad intentions; we were nudging back against the limits on us as teenagers are wont to do.

Most of my teachers were good-natured and I'm sure they knew that being strict with the good kids would alienate us and possibly prompt us to act out more. We were well aware that they knew what we were up to, and that they chose to not come down too hard on us made us respect them even more than we already did. Many of those teachers served as great mentors for me in my professional life in the same way my parents, our neighbours, and my extended family have always done so personally.

The Bizarre Bazaar

For as long as I can remember, twice a year, Hanna has had rummage sale. The only exception was during COVID-19 restrictions.

Every April and October on a Thursday and Friday, donations from people in Hanna and surrounding communities fill the curling rink and skating rink and then are sold on a Saturday. And twice a year, the damn rummage sale raises a shitload of money for the local hospital auxiliary. Over the years, the funds have enabled the local hospital to buy a mammogram machine and provide free TV in each room. And much more.

What still dumbfounds me after decades of this tradition is the amount of money that's raised: usually $20,000 to $25,000 twice a year. And it's not because the items sell for a high price. Paperback books are twenty-five cents, hardcovers are fifty cents, clothing is a dollar or two per shirt or pair of jeans. Coffee mugs are ten cents. Nice serving dishes are a dollar or two, *maybe* three. Furniture is a bigger ticket item with a sofa going for around $100, maybe a bit more. But a quarter here and a dollar there adds up when both the skating and curling rink are filled with treasures at the beginning of the day and people drive from hours away to attend and scoop up "bargoons".

The sale starts at 10:00am but by 9:30, people are already lined up at the doors. Promptly at 10:00, the doors open and the crowd spills in. It's a human stampede to the best deals. It's

Nut Bags and Num-Nums

like the rural version of door crasher Boxing Day or Black Friday sales. Everyone who has been before has a plan. As soon as the door opens, people make a beeline for their top priority table, whether it be books, dishes, furniture, toys, or tools. My favourite table? The "new" table.

The new table is where my mom last volunteered when my parents still lived on the farm. For a while she was in the toy department, but she moved to the new table after several years.

What's on the new table? New stuff! Keep in mind, "new" only means it's never been used. So, bargain hunters may find items that have been sitting on a store shelf for a few years and never moved. Shoppers may find recently produced items that are in excess at some of the local stores and donated by managers who are clearing out surplus inventory.

The best of the new table is the stuff that random people donate. We all have those "new" items stashed away in our basements or closets: wedding, birthday, anniversary, or baby gifts that were never used, stuff we bought but never needed and therefore never used, stuff we bought and forgot about, stuff we found when cleaning out our aging or dead parents' homes that they had never used. I've seen items on the new table that were forty years old and aren't manufactured any more but were still new in the box.

One of my favourite purchases from the new table was a box of highlighter pens. The box was spacious enough for twelve, but there were only nine in the box. The pens were new, so I snatched them up. Fifty cents for nine highlighters. How can you beat that?

Nut Bags and Num-Nums

I love garage sales, but I've stopped going to them over the years. I tend to buy stuff that I really don't need just because it's cheap or interesting. But the rummage sale is my one exception. It offers almost everything: furniture, tools, games, puzzles, tchotchkes, Christmas lights and ornaments for inside and out, wrapping paper, greeting cards, books, CDs, records, clothes, dishes, quilts, fabric, craft supplies, costume jewellery, household appliances, dishes, and more.

I can't walk out of the rummage sale without at least one full box of books. And if my book total ends up being something like $3.25, I hand the volunteer a $5 bill and tell them to keep the change. The money, after all, goes to the hospital in my hometown and therefore benefits former neighbours, teachers, classmates, and long-time family friends.

When my parents lived on their farm, my dad always needed jeans. Since he spent the majority of his time outside working with the cattle or in the field, he didn't care if some of his work jeans were new or had a couple of holes in them. My mom always looked for jeans for him at the rummage sale. Why pay $40 or $50 or more for a new pair when you can buy a used pair, in perfectly good condition, for fifty cents—especially when your husband only uses them for working in the barn or field?

She brought home a pair of jeans one time, in his size. Fifty cents was the going rate. Nothing wrong with these jeans at all—no holes, no stains. They had only been worn a few times. They looked new.

She tossed them at Dad for him to try on. When he came out of the bedroom to show Mom that they fit perfectly, he stuck his hands in the pockets and pulled out a $5 bill.

Nut Bags and Num-Nums

When I was staying with my parents one year for a few days, Mom came home on the Thursday night from volunteering at the rummage sale and showed us her pre-shopping treasures. (Volunteers get to pre-shop.) Among several practical items was a ceramic Herford bull, which Mom tucked under her arm when she brought it out to the kitchen to show us. This bull was a piggy bank. There was something in it but in order to find out what was inside, the bull would have to be smashed as there was no escape hatch for the piggy bank. We decided to leave it intact.

"What's the story with that?" I asked my mom.

"I had to buy it. I thought it was irresista-bull," she smirked.

I rolled my eyes.

My hilarious mother, always so prim and proper, but she does have her moments.

"I love it! What are you going to do with it?" I asked.

"Here."

She gave it to me. It proudly stands in my spare bedroom these days for visitors to enjoy.

I live an almost three-hour drive away from Hanna. If I lived close enough, I would volunteer to help collect and organize the donations, as extra help is always needed. Since I live too far way to commit to three days, I at least try to go to the sale to shop and support the cause. The sale draws shoppers from all over town but also from other communities. It's a fun social event in addition to a treasure hunt. I am guaranteed to run into former classmates and long-time family friends.

We Knew

My relationship with my mom was completely different than the one I had with my dad. She read to me when I was too young to read books, thereby teaching me to love books. Mom was "in charge"; she disciplined us, she organized our schedule, she nagged at us to do our homework and chores, and she took us to town for hobbies and shopping trips. Mom took me and Janice to church almost every Sunday; Dad usually only joined us on Easter, Mother's Day, and Christmas. When we went to The Big City (Calgary) to get new clothes for the school year or to do Christmas shopping, Dad sometimes came along but often it was just Mom who took us. She was the doer on the front lines. Mom was the bookkeeper and organizer and the person in charge of running the household. My dad was the doer behind the scenes. He was the farmer and rancher.

I spent countless hours following Dad around the farm, helping him by carrying or fetching tools, opening gates as he was moving cattle from one corral to another, doing other odd jobs, or just observing. We often spent hours together in silence. Not only were we both okay with this, but we both enjoyed the silence. In my earlier adult years, I had a friend who asked me once, "How can you and your dad go for a drive together and spend two hours in the vehicle together without ever saying a word to each other? That would drive me completely crazy!" I was never the slightest bit uncomfortable with the silence between me and my dad. We were both wired to be content and happy with silence.

Nut Bags and Num-Nums

As he aged and his dementia progressed, it became impossible to have a conversation with him. However, for as long as he was physically able to get into my vehicle, I took him for drives in the foothills southwest of Calgary. I know we both enjoyed those times of silence in the vehicle, taking in our Alberta scenery and looking at the cattle, horses, and crops with the snow-capped Rocky Mountains as a backdrop.

The same friend was incredulous at the fact that neither of my parents ever said "I love you" to me.

"Why does that matter?" I asked him. "I know my parents love me. I don't need them to say it to know it's true."

He didn't understand why I wasn't upset about never hearing those words from my parents.

I'm an actions person, not a words person. My parents worked their asses off their entire lives to build a safe, secure, and happy home for me and my sister. When times were tough, we still got treats and Christmas presents. Yes, they both smacked us, but we knew it only happened when we deserved to be disciplined.

After my mom passed away, I was leafing through a notebook she had kept beside the hospital bed she spent her last months in. There, at the back of the notebook, at some point in the last ten days of her life when she was almost always sleeping, she had obviously felt the need to put pen to paper:

Nut Bags and Num-Nums

To Janice and Lorna. I love you both very much.

It was barely legible, but there it was. The only time my mother told me she loved me. She obviously felt she needed to say it somehow in those, her final days, but I stared at those words and thought, *Wow. Mom, you didn't have to go to all that effort when you were barely alive any more. I already knew.*

But thank you.

Afterword

When I was touring around Alberta promoting my book, *Living My Golden Dream*, I went to several rural communities: Three Hills, Oyen, Brooks, Redcliffe, Bonnyville, and more. In Oyen, as I was setting up at the farmer's market, I popped across the arena to chat with the Avon lady and buy some shower gel from her.

"I'm originally from Hanna. My mom used to sell Avon, so I miss being able to get my shower gel and a few other things from her," I told the Avon lady.

"What was your mom's name?"

"Della Stuber."

She smiled.

"I knew your mom. I remember her well. She was a gem."

Gulp.

My heart welled up to hear this woman I had never met before speak so kindly of my mom, who had been dead for eleven years.

Later as I was sitting at my table, a woman stopped.

"Lorna Stuber," she looked at me, after she had seen my name on the cover of my book. "I used to know Stubers from Hanna."

"That's where I grew up! My parents farmed and ranched there for almost fifty years."

"Who are your parents?"

"Della and Harvey Stuber."

"I bought a horse from your dad."

"Oh really? Which horse was it?"

"Leo"

"I remember Leo!" I told her. "He was a calm, gentle sorrel gelding."

"Yes, he was. Are your parents still ...," her voice quieted.

"My mom passed away in 2011 but my dad is alive. He's in High River now, and I'm in Okotoks, a few minutes away from him."

She told me her name. I remembered her. She did a lot of business with my parents when I was growing up.

It had been fifteen years since my parents sold the farm and moved west, but there I was, spending the afternoon in the local arena in an area where people still remembered my parents and spoke highly of them. I have never lived in Oyen but I felt like I was home.

I feel at home when I'm in Hanna, too. One of the last times I was there before my dad died, the first place I stopped was at one of the banks. I needed to deposit some money into my dad's account, and as soon as I stepped out of my vehicle, I almost ran smack into my aunt Marg. We stopped and chatted in the parking lot for a few minutes.

"I still can't come to town without getting busted," I texted Janice moments later. "I just ran into Marg. I've literally been in town for one minute."

For years, Janice and I had a running joke that every time she or I went back to Hanna and stopped at the Texaco (which is no longer there), there was a 100 per cent chance of running into our uncle Ted and aunt Irene. We always did regardless of what time of day it was, and it always felt so random.

I feel at home in my uncle Marvin and aunt Cynthia's living room in Hanna, having a visit. By coincidence, they now live in the same crescent my mom's parents lived in after they sold the farm and moved into town. (Okay, yeah, Hanna's not that big, but still ... the same street? That's small-town.)

And I feel at home when I *am* at home, in my own house in Okotoks, chatting on the phone with my aunt Sandra. After attending high school with my mom and marrying one of my dad's brothers, she has lived in Calgary for as long as I've known her. It was her mother who taught me how to play piano and who busted me for writing a fictitious bio about Bach. It's great to be living so close together.

"Six degrees of separation"? In small-town Alberta, there is no separation. It's all first degree. If home is where the heart is, then yes, my heart is still with Hanna and its surrounding communities, especially since my parents and grandparents on my mom's side are now buried there. I don't go back often, but when I do, I soak in the prairie landscape, summer or winter.

I value the gift my parents gave me by raising me in this location. The gift of freedom to roam as a child for hours, for miles, with a horse and a dog. The gift of developing a love and appreciation for animals who serve as pets but also animals who contribute to our food source, whether they become the food or are the work animals who help grow other foods.

And the gift of community. Regardless of where I travel, no matter where I live, my feet are still grounded in this Canadian soil under this expansive, blue, Alberta sky. I greatly value the people I have known for decades—those who have known me since childhood, who remember my parents, and who still shape the person I continue to become.

Acknowledgements

Thank you dear Kimmy Beach, my editor, for The Greatest Collaboration in the History of Music™ and for the much-needed kicks in the butt. For example, "It may startle you to know that you use a version of this phrase twenty times throughout the book. The ideal number (I think) is zero." I'm still pretty sure the gleeful pigs loved me, though.

My memory isn't perfect; no one's is, and so I need to acknowledge and thank the following people for helping me fill in some gaps: Janice, Sunch, Jay, Darcy, Karen, and my uncles Roger, Marvin, and Gerry.

And thank you to everyone who is and is not mentioned in this book who has contributed to my ongoing attempt to be a well-rounded, intelligent, decent person. This book is a thank you to all who have influenced me during and since my childhood. I continue to look to you as examples of how to better myself.

About the Author

Lorna Stuber has a B.Ed. with a double major in English Language Arts and Social Studies Education (University of Lethbridge), a Dip.Ed. in ESL Curriculum and Instruction (University of Calgary), and an Editing Certificate (Simon Fraser University). She spent her twenties teaching ESL in Japan and Calgary, Canada, and her thirties and forties teaching online high school English, Social Studies, and options for the Calgary Board of Education. After resigning from her latest teaching position, she began editing, writing, and ghostwriting. Lorna spends most of her money on plane tickets and accommodation in cool and often obscure travel destinations. She has now been to almost thirty countries on all continents except Antarctica, which is definitely on the list!

When she is not helping others fine-tune their writing, Lorna is snowshoeing, volunteering for local theatre, working on her own writing, and fulfilling her duties as the self-appointed "bad-influence auntie" to her friends' kids. She currently lives in Okotoks, Canada, with her dust elephants and her kitchen view of the Rocky Mountains.

Lorna was a finalist for the 2023 Tom Fairley Award for Editing Excellence.

Website: lornastuber.com
Facebook: facebook.com/lornastubereditor
LinkedIn: linkedin.com/in/lorna-stuber-freelance-editor-writer-ghostwriter

www.ingramcontent.com/pod-product-compliance
Lightning Source LLC
Chambersburg PA
CBHW031100080526
44587CB00011B/763